HELP
WANTED

devotions
for Job Seekers

D0010981

AARON M. BASKO

JUDSON PRESS
PUBLISHERS SINCE 1824

Join our mailing list for updates and special offers.
www.judsonpress.com/mailing_list.cfm

Library of Congress Cataloging-in-Publication Data

Basko, Aaron.
    Help wanted : devotions for job seekers / Aaron Basko.
        p. cm.
    ISBN 978-0-8170-1723-1 (pbk. : alk. paper) 1. Unemployed--Religious life.
2. Job hunting--Religious aspects--Christianity. I. Title.
    BV4596.U53B37   2012
    242'.68—dc23

                                                                    2012023017

Printed in the U.S.A.
First printing, 2012.

Contents

Foreword

In today's economy, lifetime employment is almost extinct. Vocational discernment is not a one-shot thing to be undertaken on college graduation. It is a lifelong process. And I emphasize *process* because, in this extraordinary volume, Aaron Basko has crafted a holistic process of reflection, action, and spiritual development that could serve us all in the lifelong pilgrimage of finding the right fit for our daily work.

In reality there is no perfect fit in this life—that must wait for the new heaven and new earth—but Basko has set out to provide help in finding work that substantially fits our character, giftedness, values, and passions. And he does so in a way that is truly accessible to all. A certified career development counselor and member of numerous professional organizations, Basko has assisted generations of students to find suitable employment. But he offers one more commendable credential as author of this book of devotions: he shares his own job-search story, wringing this inspirational and practical book out of his personal experience.

Aaron Basko is convinced, as I am, that God is more interested in our lives than we are; that God goes before us in all of life's journeys; that God is intimately involved in the details of our lives; and that God wants us to work in a righteous way. Basko elaborates this perspective by choosing a short Scripture on which to meditate, offering a real-life application as it relates to God's purposes in our job search, and then inviting us to take a small but concrete step forward. The author approaches his subject from a Christian perspective, but there is a winsomeness in Basko's unselfconscious references to God and the people and principles of the Bible that invites all to seek transcendent meaning in our job search. It is this aspect that I find most invigorating in this slim but potent little book.

The one-time President of VISA International said we should hire and promote on the basis of integrity. Experience, he argues, is the easiest thing to get if people have the other requirements—knowledge, motivation, and above all, integrity. It is integrity that Basko sees as the deepest outcome of the divine-human conspiracy to find a good job. This process is not just about the job search but about the person who is searching. And in the challenging situation of work-search, something powerful can happen in us, to us, and for us.

So what can the job seeker gain by taking fifteen minutes a day to read and digest each of these devotional gems? First, you can gain a divine perspective on work in this world. Given by God to humankind, work is a good gift of Creation. Even looking for work (which is itself a full-time job) is good work. Second, from God's perspective there is no sacred-secular divide. So-called ministry is not more holy than making things and offering services in the world. Third, you will gain practical help in being able to present to others your capacities, goals, and gifts. Basko calls this "God's fingerprint in your life." Finally, you will experience job-seeking as a spiritual discipline—something that forms us in our relationship with a transcendent and personal God.

Will you be certain to find a wonderful job by reading this book? Perhaps. But even more important you become a job-seeker that is worth being sought—not only by a potential employer but by the Divine Headhunter who is Author and Founder of our faith. Read this fabulous resource. Inwardly digest, and stick with it to the end, and then go back and read it again—perhaps years later, the next time you find yourself walking this road of discovery again.

R. Paul Stevens
Marketplace Mentor and Author
The Other Six Days, *Doing God's Business*,
Taking Your Soul to Work, and *Work Matters*

Introduction

The phrase "Help Wanted" gives hope to job seekers everywhere as they read it online or see it on a sign, but it also describes how we can approach God during this time of transition. The goal of this book is to challenge you to look at your job search the way God views it. Rather than an awkward pause in your career that makes you panic, a job search can be a chance for God to guide you toward what you were created to do, and for God's glory to show through in your life.

The world is not always kind to job seekers. The market can be incredibly tough for new graduates looking for a first opportunity. It can be just as bad for experienced workers who lose a job or find themselves in an unsustainable situation. But I am convinced that God wants to make the most of this unique time in your life. If you know Jesus Christ, and you can trust him to guide you, your search can result in God's glory for your good.

Every journey of discovery is made up of smaller practical steps that help you reach your destination. Following each devotion you will find a section called One Small Step for Today. Each of these steps is something you can do right now either to strengthen your job search skills or to deepen your relationship with God during this season of life.

Yes, a job search can be a stressful time, but it can also be a time of great growth and exploration as the Lord teaches you more about his purpose for your life. Let the devotions in this book provide the help you want—to energize, equip, and encourage you for your big leap!

In the Hope of Glory

All this is for your benefit, so that the grace that is reaching more and more people may cause thanksgiving to overflow to the glory of God. —2 Corinthians 4:15

The world's message is that your value depends on position—your job title, annual income, and academic degree. According to this way of thinking, the job hunt is something to be ashamed of, perhaps because it suggests that you can't inspire employers to come looking for you. But why do those of us who belong to Jesus fall for this? After all, we believe that the Son of the living God died on a cross to show how much we are worth to him. Jesus did so without checking any credentials, giving up his own position in glory without regard for any of our accomplishments, or lack of them.

In an even bigger gamble, Jesus entrusted his kingdom to a ragtag group of rough fishermen, corrupt tax collectors, and religious extremists who deserted their leader right before the cross. Your résumé looks great compared to those of the twelve disciples! Why should we be ashamed of our talents, our hopes, and our efforts to discover the work for which we were created when God was willing to take such wild risks on us?

Remember the example of Jesus, who gave up a throne in heaven's glory to sojourn with us on the dusty roads of first-century Judea? Is it possible that this trying time in our professional lives, when the job market deals out plenty of black eyes, can actually become a time of triumph? Can it be a time when we hear God's voice more clearly and when God's glory shines through our situation? Romans 5:2-5 says: "We boast in the hope of the glory of God. Not only so, but we also rejoice in our sufferings, because we know that suffering produces perseverance; perseverance, character; and character, hope. And hope does not put us to shame, because God's love has been poured out into our hearts through the Holy Spirit, who has been given to us."

We can count on God's promise that we are reaping benefits from our trying time. The Romans 5 passage above may seem scary because it explains that often it is suffering that matures us and grants us unshakable hope. If you are reading this book, however, chances are you are already suffering through the challenges that come with the job hunt. Therefore, you can be sure that the "good stuff" promised in this verse—perseverance, strong character, and God's hope, which does not disappoint—is on its way if you are seeking the Lord's will as diligently as you are seeking new employment.

As you take on the challenges of the job search, be on the lookout also for what God is doing. If your eyes are open, you will see the Lord's glory shine through for your good!

One Small Step for Today

One of the first steps of a job hunt is compiling an up-to-date résumé detailing your education, skills, work history, and other experience. Imagine the great Bible heroes, such as Moses or Esther, Paul or Mary Magdalene, writing their own résumés. How would those résumés have looked before they discovered God's purpose—and then after? Now look at your own résumé. Highlight any area that may be a barrier to finding meaningful work—lack of education, experience, or skills. How might the Lord receive glory in these areas of weakness or lack?

Buried Treasure

I will give you hidden treasures,
riches stored in secret places, so that
you may know that I am the LORD.
—Psalm 112:4-5, NIV

God has quite a reputation for redeeming good things out of bad situations. The Lord's great love for us is powerful enough to transform any situation. From the terrible choice of Joseph's brothers to sell him into slavery, God made provision for many nations during a time of famine (Genesis 45:4-8). From his rejection by the world, Jesus was established as cornerstone of God's reign on earth (Matthew 21:42). From the persecution of the early church, God accomplished the spread of the gospel (Acts 8:1,4). In my own life, out of the challenges of a difficult job search, God blessed me with the words and insights for this book.

I had been in the job hunt for a while and was frustrated that things weren't moving faster. My mother, who loves devotional books and often gives them as gifts, mentioned that she had been looking unsuccessfully for a devotional that would be helpful for someone searching for a job. She joked that I should write one. I laughed at the time, but the Lord must have used her comment to plant a seed in my mind, because after that I began to see God's hand everywhere in my search. Not that I suddenly found a job— I didn't—but God sent me events and people to encourage me and help me see a bigger perspective. Somewhere along the way, it dawned on me that if I shifted my focus outward to perceive how the Lord could use this experience to bless others, I might find buried treasure.

The book of Proverbs says that "those who refresh others will themselves be refreshed" (11:25, NLT). I began to see my obstacles as opportunities to help other people. Every time the Lord taught me something about my search, I asked myself, "Is this something that someone else could use?" I wrote these thoughts down, along with the Scripture verses that encouraged me. As I explored each new thought God laid on my heart, I began to think of the words as personal gifts from the Lord to me, gifts that one day I could give to bless someone else. Years later that has come true.

The principle at work here is at the heart of many clichés: rain makes the flowers grow; when life gives you lemons, make lemonade; every cloud has a silver lining. In Matthew 12:35, Jesus says, "A good person produces good things from the treasury of a good heart" (NLT). With Christ inside you, you have all the good you need to create something meaningful from your situation. Ask God how your challenge can serve others. Maybe this is an opportunity to volunteer your time and talents or invest in neglected relationships. Maybe God is fortifying you to be someone's mentor or career counselor—take good notes! Pray for eyes to see where the Lord has hidden treasure for you; then listen for what God would have you do in response.

One Small Step for Today

Want a fun way to identify the most important aspects of your job search? Open your electronic résumé and copy the descriptive part (not the personal data) into free online "word cloud" software, such as Wordle or TagCloud. These programs create a visual picture of your information based on how frequently words appear. Do the largest words match the job descriptions you are considering? Are they the skills you want to use? If not, consider modifying your résumé to integrate words that reflect who you are and what is most important to you.

Leap Forward

> *"For I know the plans I have for you,"*
> *declares the* LORD, *"plans to prosper you*
> *and not to harm you, plans to give you*
> *hope and a future."* —Jeremiah 29:11

When I was young, I was a fan of the 1980s television show *The A-Team*. (The series later served as inspiration for a blockbuster movie.) During most episodes, as the team foiled the bad guys with their elaborate stratagems, their leader, Col. Hannibal Smith, said with a smug smile, "I love it when a plan comes together." No matter how bad the situation was, the viewer knew that Colonel Smith would have a plan and that things would work out alright in the end.

Jeremiah 29:11 assures us that God, like Colonel Smith, has a plan. And with God as our leader, we can weather even the toughest challenges—especially if we are part of a team that is committed to following the plan God provides. You may be a brand-new graduate, entering the job market during a tough time, unsure of what the future holds or which direction to go. You may have a lot of experience but suddenly find yourself laid off in the latest round of budget cuts and belt-tightening. Or you may have found yourself in a job that is poisoning your soul, and you made the difficult and risk-laden decision to resign.

It is time for action, and now you must decide whose plan you are going to follow. We all have our own plans and visions for work and for the future, and those may be good. They may be born out of the desires that the Lord has written on our hearts. At other times, our plans have more to do with earning a particular income, achieving a certain position or status, or attaining a coveted standard of living. Where our plans collide with God's purposes, we must decide if we are willing to surrender our ideas about the future and follow God's leading.

I think of my mom, whose favorite Bible verse is Jeremiah 29:11. Both she and my dad were trained as doctors, but as many women of her generation did, Mom made a difficult choice to stop practicing when they had children. For thirty-plus years, she has had what I think of as an empowerment ministry. She volunteers as a speaker, coach, and organizer for several women's organizations, and she leads multiple local Bible studies. Clearly, this was not the job she envisioned when she pursued a medical degree, but she learned to let the Lord work through her wherever she found herself.

You can have confidence in God's plan to give you "hope and a future." Psalm 138:8 agrees: "The LORD will fulfill his purpose for me" (NRSV). Your first task as a job seeker is to choose whether you will leap forward in the direction of God's plan for your life or if you will wander in the wilderness of résumés and interviews relying on your own power. Choose God's plan. Bring your plans and ideas to the Lord, and watch God transform your job search.

One Small Step for Today

Try a life-diagramming exercise to explore the plan that the Lord has already been developing in your life. (Visit the Resources page at www.aaronbasko.com for a template.) To begin, think of the most important positive experiences of your life—jobs, classes, activities, relationships, and so on. Scatter these across a sheet of paper. What made each one so meaningful? What skills were you using? What emotions or ideas emerged? Draw lines between words that seem related. List emerging themes in order of importance. What is God teaching you through your past as you plan for the future?

Divine Headhunter

*Call to me and I will answer you and
tell you great and unsearchable things
you do not know.* —Jeremiah 33:3

In the corporate job market, people often rely on individuals known colloquially as headhunters. In more professional language, they are freelance recruiters who strive to match prospective employers with potential employees.

In your job search, you may have opportunities to make contacts with recruiters, networking services, or career counselors. These can all be great resources, and God may use them to open doors for you or give you good advice. The Lord is a master at putting just the right people together for the good of everyone involved. Look for opportunities to build relationships with those who can impact your life and give you good counsel.

Ultimately, though, God is the best headhunter you could ever want. The Lord not only knows you inside and out (because, after all, our Headhunter is also our Creator), but the divine Headhunter, being omniscient, also knows the job market. The Lord knows what employers are thinking and when a position will open even before it does. In fact, God is the only headhunter I know who can actually create a position at will. God can accomplish more for us in minutes than a human headhunter can do for us in months!

Let me give you one example. My wife's graduate school costs were paid for because she worked as house manager at one of the premiere theaters in Illinois. At the time this venue, which was connected to our graduate school, only hired students who were theater majors—and my wife wasn't one of them. In fact, she knew almost nothing about theater. But, here's how it happened.

My wife had been accepted to her graduate program, but we had no idea how we would pay for it. Meanwhile, four states away, a woman resigned her job at the theater to start seminary study. Before leaving her position, she called her old college advisor to update him about her next career move. This professor also happened to be my wife's advisor at the same undergraduate college, and when the woman called, my wife happened to be in the office. When it was discovered that my wife would be relocating to study at that university near the theater, the professor made a call and the woman was able to get my wife an interview. Because the interviewer was looking for someone different from the usual theater major, suddenly my wife had a job and two years of graduate school tuition.

Who but God has the connections to make an arrangement like that? To this day this story is a reminder to us of the Lord's sovereignty. I also see it as evidence that God loves to make a great match! The Lord knows the exact circumstances that will lead us to fulfill the purpose for which we were created. Make sure you have enlisted the ultimate Headhunter to guide your career path.

One Small Step for Today

Think about the advantages God has in the "headhunting" process. Make a list of the needs you can share with the Lord that you could not share with another recruiter or employer. Talk with God about each need and commit those needs to the Lord in prayer. Then put your list in a prominent place in your job search materials to remind yourself that God is at work for you and that the divine Headhunter knows your needs even better than you do!

Give God This Day

When I am afraid, I put my trust in you.
—Psalm 56:3

One summer my family was visiting close friends in another state. When we arrived at their home in the middle of a weekday, I was surprised to find the husband, Steve, home doing yard work. "Did you take the day off just for us?" I asked.

"No, I quit my job today," he replied.

Steve had left a company a little over a year before, taking a severance package when it looked like layoffs were imminent. He quickly accepted another position, relieved to find something local during a difficult economic time. It was not a good fit, however, and a year of struggling with it had convinced both him and his employer that it was best to part ways.

My mind immediately went to the obstacles—the needs of his family, the potential damage to his résumé, the financial impact. I was worrying for him. His perspective was better. Sure he was nervous, but he believed this was best for him and his family. He felt that God had something else in mind.

He was right. Recently he told me about the new job he started with a smaller company that makes him feel like part of the family. He can actually see the impact he has on the company's bottom line, which makes the work a lot more meaningful. He feels like they care about him, and the better location and hours let him invest more time in his kids.

"I had no idea how much weight I was carrying around with me in my old job," he said. "But God did, and he knew better than I did what I needed."

Steve showed incredible trust, being willing to step forward into the unknown and let God lead. In other situations, trust is less about action and more about remaining patient under stress.

Not long ago, another good friend of mine also found herself in a tough work situation. A new boss took over the division and made working there very difficult. In her refusal to take sides in an internal squabble, my friend made herself the target of this manager's mistrust. Several of her colleagues either left or were fired, but my friend decided to stay. She felt committed to others in the office and decided to trust the Lord to work something out. Eventually the manager worked himself out of a job, but my friend continues to work there and flourish. I think she would tell you that the hardest part was not becoming bitter while waiting for the change to come.

Trust is difficult when nothing seems to be happening or when we cannot see very far ahead of us. But that is when it is really trust. Do we move or do we stay? We can haunt ourselves by constantly looking back or by visualizing future unknowns, or we can ask, "Lord, what is my assignment for today? Where do you want me today?"

One Small Step for Today

The job search can consume all your waking hours if you let it because you are never really "done" for the day. Try starting the day with one or two goals you want to accomplish, and complete those before you can be distracted by anything else. Whenever possible, group small tasks like email and phone calls at set times rather than scattering them throughout the day. At the end of the day, having completed your initial tasks, give yourself permission to be done. Offer the day to God and leave tomorrow's tasks for tomorrow. As Jesus tells us, "Tomorrow will worry about itself. Each day has enough trouble of its own" (Matthew 6:34).

Fingerprints

It is the glory of God to conceal a matter;
to search out a matter is the glory of kings.
—Proverbs 25:2

Some people benefit greatly from taking career assessments. God has given certain individuals wisdom in designing and interpreting assessments to help others discover what God has written on their hearts. Take full advantage of these resources. I have used two basic types of assessments to assist people in career exploration—skills tests and personality tests. Skills tests identify those things you enjoy doing and match those abilities with jobs with similar characteristics. Personality assessments ask who you are, what you value, and how you approach the world. Both can be useful tools, but the key is to leave room for wise counsel.

The parents of a college student contacted me to work with their son, who was struggling with career direction. I began to walk him through some of the assessments I use to look for God's handiwork. The student latched onto the answers provided by the tests and was ready to start planning his future based on those answers, but something about the results just didn't ring true for me. Based on my conversations with him, I had this nagging feeling we were missing something.

In this particular case, God had arranged it so that the student's family accompanied him when he came to take the assessment. Sometimes that can be a distraction for the person receiving career advice, but this time I felt a nudge that I should involve them. I began to ask questions of his family members, and a new picture of the student emerged. Numerous clues about what he loved and how God had equipped him came to the fore. Suddenly he could explain to me why he had chosen the major he had been pursuing and why he had tired of it once he arrived at college. Best of all, he could identify what options he was really excited about, and with a little help, he put together a plan to explore them.

It was not my wisdom that brought this young man an answer. God had made him the way he was, and God arranged for us to meet and for his family members to be present. God even nudged me before we drew the wrong conclusions. That is the thrill of the career search process. It is really the search for God's fingerprints on our lives and hearts. If we earnestly seek God's purpose, the Lord will use all sorts of tools to teach us and to draw us to it—assessments, the Scriptures, life experiences, and other people.

God is at work in your job search right now. The Lord wants you to understand what you were created for, and God wants to use you for some good purpose. As the proverb says, it is God's glory to hide a little bit of wonder and a little bit of the Lord's greatness in you, and it can be your joy to uncover it as you seek God's wisdom.

One Small Step for Today

If you have never taken a career test, consider taking one. Many well-known resources are available, such as the Strong Interest Inventory or the Campbell Interest and Skill Survey for skills, or the Myers-Briggs Type Indicator or Keirsey Temperament Sorter for personality. Whatever you choose, remember that the assessment alone does not offer all the answers. Assessments only help us more clearly see the qualities God has written into our lives. It is God who will provide the wisdom to interpret the facts and devise a plan according to a divine design.

Flex Your Joy

> *Do not grieve, for the joy of the* LORD *is your strength.* —Nehemiah 8:10

My job search had started to grow long and I was tired. My initial this-will-be-an-adventure attitude had worn off. I had done some networking and sent out a bunch of résumés. I even responded to the Spirit's nudging to explore job opportunities far afield from my education and experience, but so far—nothing. The jobs I felt I wanted didn't seem to want me. I needed a new source of strength.

This verse from Nehemiah had always puzzled me. "The joy of the LORD is your strength." It sounded like an equation, but one with a piece missing. I wanted strength, but how could I get it? It comes from the joy of the Lord. Great, but where would I find the joy? In the midst of a discouraging and prolonged job search, I couldn't see an answer.

As God continued to lead me from one job possibility to another, I bumped into this verse again and something clicked. God wasn't just moving slowly because I could not go any faster. I realized that the Lord actually liked talking with me and speaking into my life. I also recognized that I really liked conversing back, whether or not I received the answer I was anticipating.

It finally occurred to me that I was reading the verse incorrectly. It was not talking about a type of joy that belongs to the Lord that I should covet as a blessing, but about the joy of the presence of the Lord. It is the kind of joy that wells up within my spirit when I experience merely being with the Lord, experiencing the person and presence of God. This joy, and the strength that comes with it, is not something God gives or withholds. It is something we absorb from spending time with God.

As this dawned on me, my question started to change from "Lord, what is the final answer to my job question?" to "Lord, what do you want to show me today?" As I tried on new job possibilities, I realized that I was equipped to do lots of things if God said the word, and that took some of the pressure off. I started writing down what we talked about in my prayer times, and I made note of the small gifts and insights that God seemed to leave for me everywhere.

I still worked like crazy. I continued to network and to investigate any new possibility the Lord revealed because I never knew when this would be the one. But now I was reinvigorated because I was no longer trying to wrestle the answers out of God. Now the Lord and I were walking the path together.

Finally the right job did come. God opened a door into a great new career, and the Spirit was kind enough to tell me, in the quiet of my heart and through good guidance, "This is it." But the mystery revealed in this verse was the bigger prize.

In any job search, you will face challenges, but God will minister to you in a thousand small ways, nourishing your soul with the Spirit's presence. Whatever happens in your career, now or in the future, you can know that when you seek the Lord's presence, you will also find joy to strengthen you on the journey.

One Small Step for Today

Discovering the joy of the Lord's presence is not about hearing the dramatic voice in the moment of crisis. Involve God in the small, seemingly insignificant decisions of daily life, and give the Lord permission to take you outside of your I-must-find-the-answer thinking. The job search offers you countless opportunities to practice. Should you send the résumé or not, make the call or not, follow up or not? Ask. Start a conversation with God and see where it leads.

Neon Signs

*Let the morning bring me word of your
unfailing love, for I have put my trust in
you. Show me the way I should go, for
to you I entrust my life.* —Psalm 143:8

Have you ever wished that God would just make his will clear?
You want to know where to look for a position. You are seeking
the right field with the right employer, doing work you can feel
good about. You get an offer and think you should accept it, but
how can you be sure?

Growing up, my family had a prayer tradition. When the decision got really big and the answer was not clear, we prayed for a
"neon sign." I can't remember where the phrase originated, but
we used it only when we felt we clearly needed God to speak on
an issue. We would pray, "Lord, we want to follow you in this
situation. We don't want to head in the wrong direction. Please
send us a neon sign. Make it big enough and bright enough that
we can't miss it."

A "neon sign" was a great visual for me as a kid. And I can't
recall a time when we made that request that God did not respond in an unmistakable way. The Lord always seemed to honor
our desire to be faithful.

One of my pivotal experiences was a year-long exchange program in which I lived with host families and attended high school.
I wanted to study in Spain, but the organization I was working
with ran out of spots in Spain and offered me Argentina. This was
a year of my life we were talking about, and making this choice
would interrupt my future plans. I wasn't sure I wanted to risk it

by going somewhere I knew nothing about. I had never even met anyone from Argentina.

I prayed about it, asking for that neon sign, and a couple of weeks later the Lord responded. I attended a large church conference in my area. The evangelist Luis Palau was the main speaker. Reading his bio at the event, I realized he was from—you guessed it—Argentina! I had the chance to speak to him about my dilemma after a session, and he said, "You should go." That was as close to neon as I could want.

The Lord knew how that experience would change my life. There God spoke to me in a way he never had while I was in my home environment. The experience also prepared me for future career opportunities as I learned Spanish, practiced my cross-cultural skills, and enjoyed an international internship, all of which made me a more attractive candidate to employers. Knowing how important that year would be, God was gracious enough to grant a neon sign to guide me.

I still need neon signs sometimes. I'm glad the Lord humors my small steps of faith. God is gracious to us when our frail human spirits tremble. When you need clear direction from the Lord, ask. God is faithful to answer.

One Small Step for Today

Think back to when the Lord has sent you signs that changed the course of your life. Did you acknowledge and thank God for them? Do so again now. Ask for clearer sight to see the subtler signs God may be sending you in this phase of your job search. If you need a neon sign about a decision right in front of you, ask for it—not for your convenience, but out of a sincere desire to follow God's leading.

The Path of Life

You have made known to me the path of life; you will fill me with joy in your presence, with eternal pleasures at your right hand. —Psalm 16:11

What is the path of life that God makes known to us? What is the secret? Isn't it answered in the next part of the verse? "You fill me with joy in your presence, with eternal pleasures at your right hand." Where do I find life and joy? In God's presence. Where do I find blessing? Near the Lord.

Recently I have made a connection between discovering the path of life in God's presence with the apostle Paul urging in Ephesians 6:18 to "pray in the Spirit on all occasions"; it is an exhortation echoed in 1 Thessalonians 5:17: "Pray continually." How many of us see those verses and say, "Okay, so I should pray more often" or "I need daily prayer time"? What if Paul actually meant something more significant and far more literal? Could he possibly have meant exactly what he said: "Pray continually"?

I have been a Christian since I was nine years old, but not until my twenties did I decide that I wanted to follow Jesus wholeheartedly. Shortly after that time, I was promoted to a new position with greater responsibilities and a new office location. I remember inviting Jesus to come with me into that new place and make it his own. Wow! What a response. For some reason, there was an extra desk in my office, and throughout the day I would try to picture the Lord sitting at it. His presence was so real. I remember thinking, "I am sitting across the desk from the King of kings, and I can ask any question I want at any time! I have full and complete access to Jesus." I have not always maintained that focus of staying "online" with Christ, but since that day, it has been my desire to do so.

What would it be like to speak to God throughout the day, not just in your "quiet time," but in your times of activity? What would it be like to be "online" with Jesus as much as possible? This transition time might just be the right time to find out.

One Small Step for Today

How often do you check your email or surf the Web, whether at your computer or via a tablet or smartphone? Shouldn't we be even more eager in our contact with God? Why not make it your habit to connect with God briefly every time you do something online? Whenever you open your email or a browser, take a moment to acknowledge God. Offer a word of praise or thanksgiving, and invite God into whatever you are planning to do. Stay connected with God throughout your day so that the Lord can show you the "path of life."

Trust Training

> *Trust in the LORD with all your heart*
> *and lean not on your own understanding;*
> *in all your ways submit to him, and he*
> *will make your paths straight.*
> —Proverbs 3:5-6

A good friend of mine has been pretty successful as a financial adviser and now owns his own company. Andy has a remarkable commitment to Jesus Christ and gives generously of his time serving his church. He projects integrity and strength. Other people see these qualities and respond to him. When I first met him, I couldn't figure out what was different about him. A few months later, he mentioned that he had been a Marine, and he told me a bit about his experience. Then the pieces clicked. He acts like a person whose qualities have been tested.

Andy doesn't have a swagger or give off a tough-guy air at all. His back just seems straighter than the backs of most people, and he seems more comfortable with himself. I know that his time in military training and active duty was grueling and pushed him to test his limits and adjust his values. He has shared with me that the discipline he learned helped him through the difficulties of starting a civilian career in the financial field, in which he had no previous experience. He lives like someone who has walked into the desert with God and walked out stronger and with better perspective. God used his military training to prepare him to live a more effective civilian life.

God may be using this time of transition as training for the trust you will need throughout your career. If you are open to it, you will learn who you are in a way that will serve you for years to come. Many factors are beyond your control, making it an excellent time for God to get your attention and win your trust. God deserves our trust from the beginning, but when we are most dependent, the Lord's glory shines the brightest. Then, when our Champion delivers an answer, the experience creates a monument to God's trustworthiness. When other problems come in daily life, we can look back and recount how God led us to a job just as the Israelites recounted their rescue from Egypt.

This job search may give you the opportunity to learn the most important skill of all: reliance on God. Use this time to lay the groundwork for a relationship built on trust. Even when you find a job you love, you will have times of stress and uncertainty. The Lord is our rock and will provide us with stability and guidance. Learn to put yourself in God's hands—now and throughout your career.

One Small Step for Today

Trust does not come naturally. One natural way to exercise your trust muscles during the job search is to let God guide the application process. As you read job postings and decide where to send your résumé or put in an application, ask the Holy Spirit to nudge you about where to apply. As you put together your materials, commit each opportunity to the Lord, praying that the Holy Spirit will open only the right doors. Daily renew your promise to trust God's guidance.

Time to Work

> *I know that there is nothing better for*
> *[workers] than to be happy and enjoy*
> *themselves as long as they live; moreover,*
> *it is God's gift that all should eat and*
> *drink and take pleasure in all their toil.*
> —Ecclesiastes 3:12-13, NRSV

Until recently I considered the book of Ecclesiastes to be the most depressing book in the Bible. The biblical author begins by declaring, "Utterly meaningless! Everything is meaningless!" (1:2), and a common subject he addresses is work. "What do people get for all the toil and anxious striving with which they labor under the sun? All their days their work is grief and pain; even at night their minds do not rest. This too is meaningless" (2:22-23).

Pretty depressing stuff, right? And yet there is another layer to the words. In 2:24 the author continues by saying, "A person can do nothing better than to eat and drink and find satisfaction in their own toil," and in 3:13 he suggests that such satisfaction is a gift from God. In 3:22 he reiterates, "There is nothing better for a person than to enjoy their work, because that is their lot."

So what is work: "grief and pain" or "a gift from God"?

When I read the section again, I noticed that the Teacher (whom tradition associates with King Solomon) does not seem to be critiquing work itself so much as the time and effort people invest in a desperate attempt to build something that will outlast them. The issue is our human "toil and anxious striving" and the worrisome ambition that won't allow us to sleep.

With this I began to see some of the true wisdom of Ecclesiastes. Work is not meant to be on our minds every moment of the day. It is not meant to be our monument to ourselves at the end of our lives. Work is not what proves who we are—it is simply a part of the life given to us at Creation and a tool used to shape us in God's image.

When I think about the need to keep a right relationship with work, I think of my dad, a small-town doctor who bypassed several opportunities to expand his business. Why? For several reasons I admire. First, he decided that one-on-one interaction with his patients was most important to him. Second, remaining a single-doctor practice allowed him to make his office a Christ-infused ministry to many people. Third, especially during the years when my sister and I were young, Dad was able to flex his hours. He worked later into the evening than some other dads, but he also worked a modified weekly schedule. We could count on him to be available at his scheduled times off. Our dinnertime was a little later than most people ate, but he was there with us. He found ways to be very effective while still keeping his priorities intact.

My dad knew what the author of Ecclesiastes taught: everything has its time (3:1-8). Work too has an appropriate time and seasons—and it is not all day every day. As you enter your next season of work, know what you believe about it, and learn to accept God's gift.

One Small Step for Today

A job search can be a tough time to keep your balance between doing what is necessary and obsessing every waking moment. A job search schedule is a good tool for finding the balance between staying on task and avoiding anxious obsession. A search schedule briefly outlines what job search activities you will complete during the week; for example, on Mondays review the Sunday classifieds and research positions; on Tuesdays send out résumés. Create a schedule for your weekly goals, or use the sample in the resources section at www.aaronbasko.com.

Armor Up

Therefore put on the full armor of God,
so that when the day of evil comes, you
may be able to stand your ground, and
after you have done everything, to stand.
—Ephesians 6:13

My beliefs have likely cost me at least one job opportunity. During an interview, my potential employer asked what seemed like casual questions about some of the articles I have written for Christian students about the college and career process. I didn't think anything of it. The rest of the interview seemed to go well, but a couple of days later, one of my references called and told me the organization had peppered him with questions about my beliefs. Was I too conservative? Ironically, this was—at least historically—a church-affiliated organization. My reference was not a Christian, but he found himself in the strange position of defending my faith!

Here is my word of advice: Go with your armor on. As you search for the place where God will use you, remember that there are principalities and powers who don't want you trespassing on their territory. Whether you sell shoes or stocks, fix cars or teeth, you step on the battlefield to do it. Your enemy is also in the work world, and he will use people, policies, and power to keep God from getting glory from your life. Clothe yourself daily in the spiritual armor described in Ephesians 6.

Once you are clothed in Christ's righteousness and truth, shod with the gospel of peace, and bearing faith as a shield, stand ready to carry Christ's light into the darkness. You have the helmet of salvation and the sword of the Spirit as your defense. Keep your eyes always on what is unseen—the work of the kingdom and the movement of the Spirit. Speak up for what is right. Extend radical forgiveness. Love the unlovely. Ask tough questions that make people think, and then let others come to their own conclusions. Show grace to everyone, just as unbelievable grace was shown to you—because, after all, the people around you are not the enemy. They are, like you and me, more of the world's walking wounded, whom Jesus came to rescue and restore.

As you are searching for a new position, ask God to shine light into any darkness around positions you are considering. The Lord knows what battles you will be fighting in a particular place and which ones you can handle. God provides the armor and prepares the way ahead of you.

One Small Step for Today

Riding in the car is a great time to pray through the armor of Ephesians 6. As you travel, whether to an interview or job fair or on routine errands, ask for Christ's righteousness to protect your heart and for your feet to be firmly planted in the Good News. Ask the Holy Spirit to help you take up the shield of your faith against doubts, fears, and worries. Let the knowledge of your salvation focus your mind, and recall Scriptures that will keep you on your guard. Putting on your spiritual armor will make you ready to take on whatever surprises may come today.

Professional Development

I will praise the LORD, *who counsels me;*
even at night my heart instructs me.
—Psalm 16:7

Some people enter your life as relative strangers, but through God's arrangement, they impact your professional development for life. A man named Paul did that for me. Paul was British, lured to the United States by an undergraduate soccer scholarship. When he graduated, he stayed with the college, working for the admissions office to recruit students. I was one of those students.

My first encounter with Paul was a phone call that came when I was a senior in high school. I picked up the receiver and heard this great British accent on the other end, asking me if I had heard of the college he worked for and if I would be willing to meet with him the next day at my high school. I said yes, and my adventure started. Paul and I met the next day, and he convinced me to apply for a scholarship at his institution. I won one of the scholarship spots. Paul came to the honors assembly at my school to present the award.

That fall I went off to college, where I had a great experience, but I did not see much more of Paul. Not long after I started classes, he left to pursue his passion, starting a youth soccer league. I assumed that was the end of our shared story. It was, until after I completed a graduate degree but found myself without a career plan. I thought a lot about how much I had enjoyed the college environment and wondered if higher education might be a good field for me. I thought and prayed about it, and one name came to my mind: Paul.

I tracked Paul down and called him. I'm sure it must have been a shock for him to hear from me, but he gave me great advice that has stuck with me to this day: "Aaron, you should try college admissions. The wonderful thing about admissions is that either you fall in love with it or it teaches you what you truly love." Again, his words at a pivotal moment changed my career.

He was right. Admissions taught Paul that what he loved was teaching soccer; it has taught me that what I love is helping people with their professional development. This man that I really knew so little about had shaped the course of my life twice. That would seem strange to most people, but I know the one who arranged it!

We all need people like Paul. When they speak into our lives, they are reflecting God's role as career counselor, developing us both personally and professionally. Who better to consult with on matters of life-changing importance? Jesus tells us that the Holy Spirit is available as our Counselor, and we are blessed when the Spirit chooses to work through someone like Paul.

Psalm 73:23-24 says, "Yet I am always with you; you hold me by my right hand. You guide me with your counsel." Imagine a parent holding a small hand as a child learns to cross the street. You need that kind of guidance, especially as you seek direction for the future. Reach out to the Holy Spirit for counsel. Your next conversation may change the direction of your life!

One Small Step for Today

Today reach out and thank the people who have made a difference in your life. What would it mean to them to know the impact God allowed them to have on you? Now consider whether there is someone in your life whom you might be able to counsel. A job search may not seem like a good time to coach someone else, but sharing your experience and wisdom will lift your spirits and bring life into perspective. "Freely you have received; freely give" (Matthew 10:8).

Battling "Me Vision"

> *Therefore encourage one another and build each other up, just as in fact you are doing.* —1 Thessalonians 5:11

Anytime we are in the midst of dramatic life changes, it is tempting to become egocentric. We are sure that the whole universe is waiting anxiously for us to find the answer to our problems. I sometimes feel that when my personal drama is unfolding, everyone else has somehow frozen in time and I am the only one moving. This is an acute form of tunnel vision I call "me vision."

Job searching tends to activate "me vision." The search looms so large that it is hard to see around or over it. So much seems to depend on finding a job that other priorities and other people get pushed out of the picture. Even if we set God as the compass for our efforts, we can easily focus on "God's plan for me" rather than on "where I fit into God's plan."

Not only is "me vision" a selfish way to see the world; it can be downright dangerous to our mental health. Just as when a person stares too long into the desert and begins to see mirages, the same thing happens when we become totally engrossed in our problems. By staring at them, we make them grow. The job search may become apparent proof of whether our past efforts had value, and our self-esteem may plummet into depression and despair.

In the fight against "me vision," very few weapons are as powerful as good soul friends who know you and can strengthen you with their faith. When my ego has made my problems the center of the world, I make it a point to talk with my friend Jerry. Jerry and his wife, Vivian, have been missionaries for many years, first internationally and now on college campuses as they mentor and train college students to go into the mission field.

The best thing about Jerry is that he loves Jesus more than anyone I know and wants to understand what God is doing in his life. This combination gives him the ability to speak the truth to me when I really need to hear it. A couple of years ago, I had to make a major career decision in a short amount of time under a lot of pressure. Afterward I second-guessed my decision, wondering if I had passed up an opportunity to do something of eternal significance. I obsessed over it for weeks. When I finally mentioned it to Jerry, he laughed and said, "You should have asked me. I could have told you right away that was a bad match for you." Immediately my cloud of anxiety lifted and I could see beyond myself again.

Who can speak like that into your life? In your job search, it is essential to have other believers who can help you break the grip of "me vision." When you are too self-focused to hear God's voice, these friends can speak for him and remind you that you are not the center of the universe.

One Small Step for Today

A key component of every job seeker's portfolio is a support network of friends and family that keep him or her both accountable and encouraged. Cultivate this support network in the same way you cultivate your references. Choose people whom you know will build you up but also give you their honest opinion when you need it. Keep in good contact with your network, especially when the process of job hunting seems to be absorbing you. As Proverbs 17:17 says, "A friend loves at all times, and kinsfolk are born to share adversity" (NRSV).

Choose Your Weapons

> *David said to the Philistine, "You come against me with sword and spear and javelin, but I come against you in the name of the LORD Almighty, the God of the armies of Israel, whom you have defied."* —1 Samuel 17:45-46

Have you been face-to-face with doubt, discouragement, rejection, or worry? Do they threaten to bury you? Sometimes the job search process seems like a towering giant—one who has been armed by the devil and is intent on pulling you away from trusting God. The enemy does not want witnesses to God's control over your situation.

God gives us a two-part strategy to bring down a giant. The first step is selecting the right weapon—and I'm not talking about a sword or even a slingshot. In 1 Samuel 17, David offers to fight the giant Goliath, but King Saul thinks David does not have enough experience (a message familiar to many job hunters). In reply, David recounts his victories over wild animals that attacked his flocks and then declares, "The LORD who rescued me from the paw of the lion and the paw of the bear will rescue me from the hand of this Philistine" (verse 37).

David armed himself by remembering times in the past when the Lord had saved him. Remembrance as a spiritual strategy can be seen throughout the Bible; it has long been used by God's people to fortify themselves in times of trial. Remembrance forms the foundation of the Jewish Passover, where each element of the ritual meal commemorates an aspect of Israel's deliverance from Egypt. Remembrance is also the heart of Christian Communion, which Jesus told us to rehearse until he comes again.

God has given me a number of these times to remember. For example, when I am most tempted to worry about finances, the Holy Spirit reminds me of the first two years of my marriage. Shortly after getting married, my wife and I both started graduate school. We moved away from family and friends and rented what we could afford—a cheap basement apartment with no furniture of our own. We had no money. We weren't sure how we'd pay for decent meals, much less for our schooling. But God arranged a fellowship for me that covered our meager living expenses and an assistantship for my wife that paid for her schooling. Our life wasn't easy. We lived on macaroni and cheese and drove a little car that leaked oil everywhere. When I finished my degree, I took the only work I could find—a sales job I was particularly bad at. (When I left, I had made so few sales that I owed the company money!) But my wife and I grew closer to each other and to God.

Best of all, this experience created an indelible monument to God's faithfulness. The Lord demonstrated beyond all doubt that he could provide for us even when we could not provide for ourselves. Like David, when I look into the past, I see God's hand at work in my life, even when doubts and fears have kept me from seeing clearly in the present. Remembrance of that past faithfulness becomes both my armor and my weapon in order to face today's giants.

One Small Step for Today

What were the moments you can remember when God really provided for you? Write them on an index card or sticky note and post them on your mirror, dashboard, or computer—anyplace where you will see them frequently. Instead of being discouraged or defensive when your job search is faltering, take heart and remember God's past faithfulness to you.

Victory Is the Lord's

All those gathered here will know that it is not by sword or spear that the L ORD saves; for the battle is the L ORD's, and he will give all of you into our hands.
—1 Samuel 17:47

Once properly armed, we can attach our reputation and our future to the Lord. That's the second part of God's strategy for battling life's giants. We must believe in the Lord's ability to deliver us. David did not rely on Saul's armor, nor did he try to find a bigger or better weapon than his enemy. Based on past experience, David knew he had the tools he needed for victory—mostly because in that moment, as in the past, David knew the Lord Almighty was with him in the struggle.

When I help students with career planning, I see many of them crushed when they face their first giant. The students are equipped with a good education; they have done their research and started to network; they have developed a professional résumé and cover letter. That's often when a well-meaning relative or friend comes along and says, "What are you going to do with a degree in that?" or "Do you have a job lined up yet?"

Those expectant and well-meaning questions often have the effect of deflating the students' hope and confidence. Almost before the students have begun, they are facing down the giant of discouragement.

If you are job searching, my guess is that you have already met this giant. It is in moments of discouragement that you need to follow David's example. Tell your loved ones that God has the situation covered. Let them know that you and the Lord are working together to find the right place for you. Say something like, "My job is to keep knocking on the doors. I'm relying on God to open the right one for me when I come to it." Instead of letting the giant put you on the defensive, say, "Thanks for asking. I know God's got it under control for me, and it would be great if you'd be on the lookout for the Lord's provision as well."

David declares what his victory will mean: proof that "there is a God in Israel" (1 Samuel 17:46). God's reputation is on the line, not ours. David was willing to risk his own future to prove that Yahweh was God, the ruler of all. Are you willing to risk your future and your reputation by pinning them to the Lord's plan? Remember that God's glory is revealed for your good!

One Small Step for Today

Discouragement is one of the biggest challenges that job seekers face. Learn to recognize it coming before it hits you. Plan now how you will respond when someone asks a question that makes you feel vulnerable and tempts you not to trust in God's provision. In most cases, the person is not trying to undermine your confidence, so your reply can be kind but firm. Jot down a couple of possible responses so that you will be ready to reassert your confidence in the Lord!

Speedy Delivery

The human mind plans the way,
but the LORD *directs the steps.*
—Proverbs 16:9, NRSV

About ten years ago, I began hiring people in my job as a manager in higher education. Since then I have noticed a pattern. God brings me exactly whom I need when I need that person—but not much before. It is amazing how often I have thought, *How will I ever fill this vacancy?* or *How can we possibly tackle this new project?* only to find that the right person appears on the doorstep as if the Lord has just sent me a really big overnight package.

I still worry about getting the right staff, but it is always a thrill when I sense that God has arranged a match. I have found employees who seem to have average skills until they begin work. Suddenly I discover there is a big *S* on their chests and they leap tall buildings in a single bound. At other times, experienced workers whose career paths look like a game of Chutes and Ladders somehow find me through strange connections.

Our Creator is amazing at fitting the right person for the right place. God is a master craftsman who has a deep toolbox. If we are willing to become an instrument in the Lord's hand, we often find ourselves moved to the right work site. Isn't that a comfort?

The best news in this for the job seeker is that I'm not the only boss in need of just the right person to show up at the right time or the only boss looking for someone to be the solution to my problems. Prospective employers are out there right at this moment looking for you; they just don't know it yet. Trust me, someone is looking for you.

Don't be discouraged that your résumé doesn't match the exact description, and don't give up if your logical steps and plans aren't getting the results you want. The Lord will determine your steps if you allow it, and in my experience God will often do so by preparing a need that you were created to fill. Somewhere a manager is saying, "Who can help me with this?" The Lord may have arranged the problem so that you can be the solution.

One Small Step for Today

The best marketing strategy is to advertise a product based not on its features (the car is red with a good sound system) but on its benefits (it will impress your friends). You want to demonstrate that your product is a solution to someone's problem. In the job market, *you* are the product that can solve an employer's problem. Use this formula to market yourself in your résumé and in response to common interview questions: Describe how your features (strong work ethic, proven leadership) produce crucial benefits (any project you give me will be done on time), and provide proof (I saved my last company $10,000 on just one project). Think about the types of problems your target company faces and be ready to show that you are the solution!

Fun at the Fork in the Road

> [The Lord] *guards the course of the just*
> *and protects the way of his faithful ones.*
> *Then you will understand what is right*
> *and just and fair—every good path.*
> —Proverbs 2:8-9

I love the original 1979 film *The Muppet Movie.* One of my favorite scenes is when Kermit and Fozzy are driving their old Studebaker cross-country. They sing "Movin' Right Along" as they start their trip, heading for fame and fortune. A few minutes into the drive, Kermit pulls out the map and says, "Hey Fozzy, I want you to turn left if you come to a fork in the road."

"Yes, sir, turn left at the fork in the road," replies the bear. A moment later he calls, "Kermiiiit!"

"I don't believe that," Kermit says as the car passes a huge fork standing in the road.*

We do encounter forks in the road (although they aren't typically six-feet-tall utensils). You are almost certainly facing one or more now. The decisions you make to apply or not to apply for a particular job and whether to accept or decline a job offer will change the path of your life dramatically. Fear that a decision may send you in the wrong direction can be paralyzing. Remind yourself that you face forks in the road every day with many small decisions. It is more likely that the accumulation of these small decisions, rather than one large one, will have the greatest impact on the overall direction of your life. Do not see every fork

---

*Kenny Ascher and Paul Williams, *The Muppet Movie*, directed by James Frawler, Walt Disney Pictures, 1979.

as a potential threat. Some of them are opportunities and can even be (*gasp!*) fun.

Typically career choices are not between right and wrong, ethical and unethical, but between one unknown path and another. Ultimately, what Fozzy and Kermit teach us is that the most important part of navigating life's forks in the road is choosing the right companion. Jesus offers to walk the road with us and to enrich our journey with his company. Our task is to learn to walk with him rather than racing off ahead and then refusing to stop and ask for directions.

We can also be assured that even if we do take a wrong turn on the journey, Jesus is better than any high-tech GPS at recalculating our route. We may even find that the inadvertent detour offers a scenic vista into our character—or God's. Our job is to trust Jesus' navigation through each step of the journey. As Jesus instructed his disciples, the Holy Spirit "will glorify me because it is from me that he will receive what he will make known to you" (John 16:14).

In the scope of your life, this time of searching and transition is a very small part. Years from now you will probably remember few of the concerns you have right now, but you will remember Christ's faithful companionship. Accept his invitation. As Kermit discovered, getting there can be half the fun if we share the journey with a trusted friend. Jesus is the best there is!

One Small Step for Today

Think about your last great road trip or other undertaking. You probably took some risks and sacrificed some comforts along the way. Good company and a sense of discovery transform a long trip into an adventure. While there were undoubtedly moments of seriousness and struggle, you also discovered times of joy and intimacy. If you make Jesus your traveling companion on this job search, you can count on his comfort in the challenges and joy in the journey.

Elevator Speech

Always be prepared to give an answer to everyone who asks you to give the reason for the hope that you have. But do this with gentleness and respect. —1 Peter 3:15

As part of the career class I teach, I require my students to attend a job fair. Before they go, in order to prepare for the conversations they will have there, I have them create a "sixty-second commercial" (also called an elevator speech). The idea is for a job seeker to give a succinct self-introduction and brief synopsis of job goals at any time, even in the minute it would take to talk with an executive between floors on an elevator.

In a job fair setting—unlike in most college or job interviews— it is up to the job candidate to initiate a conversation. If you approach the table and stand there waiting for the person behind the table to start talking, you are likely to experience a few awkward moments of silence. Instead, job seekers can introduce themselves with their name, the degrees or experience they have, and what type of position they are seeking. I require my students to script and memorize such an introduction and then to practice saying it naturally. Most of them think the assignment is silly—until they return from their first job fair, that is.

In the Bible verse above, Peter gives us instructions to prepare something very similar to an elevator speech as a way of sharing our faith in daily life. He instructs us to think out ahead of time what we will share when someone asks us why we have hope. One of my former bosses was a great example of this. Shortly after he was hired, he and I were talking about his plans for our office. I asked him, "What would you say your management style is?" He didn't even hesitate before declaring, "I try to follow the example of Jesus." He went on to give me examples, but I was still catching up. I had not even known he was a believer, but I knew we were in an environment that was not always very open to this kind of discussion.

I learned two things from him at that moment. First, I realized that my question had given him permission to speak freely. As Peter counsels, we must share the truth "with gentleness and respect," and the best way to do this is to invite people to ask questions about what is important to you. When someone asks you a personal question of this type, it signals that they are open to learning and will be more likely to receive what you have to say.

Second, I saw that knowing ahead of time what you want to say in such a moment makes all the difference. My boss had obviously thought about his management style. He knew exactly who he was and what he wanted to say about himself, and his clarity was powerful.

What is true about our professional preparation is true about spiritual readiness as well. Whether your next conversation is professional or personal, be prepared with a clear and memorable answer. You want to be ready when the Spirit creates a window for networking or opens a door to share your faith. In either case, God is at the heart of your answer.

One Small Step for Today

Write out two elevator speeches, your professional one and your spiritual one. Your spiritual introduction should describe briefly who God is to you and the difference the Lord makes in your life. Keep it short, but make sure you include a question that invites a response (for example, What does your company look for in candidates for this position?). Practice both speeches so that you can answer naturally but still get across what is most important to you. Always be ready to use them.

Ask, Seek, Knock

For everyone who asks receives, and everyone who searches finds, and for everyone who knocks, the door will be opened.
—Luke 11:10, NRSV

My friend Jay is a commercial pilot. Since we were in seventh grade, he had told us he would be a pilot, but I'm not sure I ever took his dream seriously. Flying a large airplane seemed a long way from our small town, and being a pilot was one of those things you say as a kid when you are trying to think of something impressive—like being an astronaut or the president. And although I didn't know it as a child, becoming a pilot is a career path for people with patience. As I learned from watching Jay, it can take a long time to earn your wings. Jay studied aviation in college and had to build up flight time to even be considered. Then he worked for years at small regional airports in different capacities to prove himself. Jay made a lot of sacrifices of time and money to get to his dream.

When we were just goofy kids, I had no idea that Jay's commitment ran that deep or that he would be so persistent in pursuing his passion. Jesus commends that kind of persistence. In Luke he tells two persistence parables: about the friend who asks to borrow bread in the middle of the night (11:5-8) and about the persistent widow pleading before a corrupt judge (18:1-8). In both of these stories the hero does not give up but keeps asking until an answer comes. Even flawed human beings will give in to such persistence, Jesus points out. Then why wouldn't God (who is good and just) respond to our persistence with goodness and justice?

How many times have we prayed for something once or twice and then given up and said, "Oh well, I guess it must not be God's will." But look at what Luke 18:1 records: "Then Jesus told his disciples a parable to show them they should always pray and not give up."

The Lord may have given you, like my friend Jay, a passion or a dream. Don't give up if the road is long. Pray about it and seek God's will persistently. You may not earn your wings right away. It may take a lot of persistence. You may have to log hours in the next-step job before you attain the dream career, but take Jesus' challenge to heart: ask, seek, and knock. And don't be so surprised when God's provision allows you to soar!

One Small Step for Today

When you are on the job hunt, get used to asking good questions. Prepare yourself with three to five questions for each segment of your interview process (that is, if you will meet with three groups of interviewers, bring at least twelve questions); some may be answered in the natural course of the interview, and others may become irrelevant. Focus your questions on the values and goals of the environment and your fit with it rather than on practical employee benefits. Ask what they are hoping the successful candidate will bring to the position and the workplace.

Put Down Your Roots

So then, just as you received Christ Jesus
as Lord, continue to live your lives in him,
rooted and built up in him, strengthened in
the faith as you were taught, and overflow-
ing with thankfulness. —Colossians 2:6-7

I was walking in the yard, grudgingly impressed. More than a year
ago, I had cut down our gum tree. I had cut the stump low, but
apparently I should have pulled it out. Little green shoots—twenty or more of them—were poking up all around the stump. A
week earlier, I had pulled out an equal or greater number. Every
few feet along the path of its roots, the tree was trying to rise
again. Impressive. When your root system is strong, life runs deep
and persists, despite trauma.

That resilient gum tree comes to mind when I read Colossians
2:6-7. The *New Living Translation* explains its sense of constant
nourishment with the image of letting our "roots grow down"
deep into God's love. For the believer, the source of life is God's
love and power. In fact, the whole world depends on the Lord's
love and power for its survival. Without God, our Creator, there
is no sun, no water, no air, no vegetation—no life.

God is also the source of each human life. As King David described it in Psalm 139:13, "You created my inmost being; you
knit me together in my mother's womb." God continues to nourish us throughout our lives, strengthening us and providing us
with spiritual food. We need to sink our roots down deep in the
soil of God's love. Doing so provides us with stability and renew-
al, and that gives us power to keep faith with the Lord through

tough times. Prayer, devotional time, and worship become the air, water, and sunlight that connect us to God's nourishing power.

The concept of being rooted deeply in Christ was incredibly helpful to me during my job search. I spent so much energy investigating and trying to solve the vocational puzzle that I was easily exhausted. I found that the harder I concentrated on the challenge, the bigger it grew. Conversely, the more I prayed, praised, and focused on God, the easier it was to keep things in perspective. I prayed that I could sink my roots deeper into God's love, and I took time out from my search to be with other Christians. Even when I was most discouraged, I knew I could go to God for nourishment and refreshment—roots sunk deep into Christ's living water.

One Small Step for Today

Relationships grow deep when you can just enjoy someone else's company without trying to get something out of the friendship. Grow your roots with God in the same way. Spend some time in the Lord's presence each day just being with him without asking for anything. In the short term, this will give you a break from the stresses and strains of the job search by allowing you to relax and enjoy God's company. And hopefully this new discipline will become a lifelong habit of speaking with the Lord conversationally and being quiet in God's presence.

Work It Out

It is God who arms me with strength and keeps my way secure. He makes my feet like the feet of a deer; he causes me to stand on the heights. —Psalm 18:32-33

What do you believe about work? What is its purpose? Your job search is a perfect time to find out. Most people do not have a developed philosophy of work. Some define their jobs as advancement. But what happens when success is frustrated, when these people go unrecognized, or when they stop advancing? For others, work is "just a job," a temporary prison they submit themselves to for a few hours a day in return for a paycheck. Others enjoy their jobs because they work for a cause and make a difference, but the season comes when the mission fades or the organization fails. What is missing in all these cases is a belief about work—all work—that helps us to find meaning and purpose across job descriptions.

It is true that some jobs will be a better fit for you, and you will be more satisfied if you use skills that God built you to use. But your job will never answer the questions only God can answer—who you are, what your purpose here is, how you should live.

Before you make a job change, know what work means to you. Work was never intended to be the measure of who a worker is. Our workplaces are simply places where we can practice the skills and abilities our Creator has given us. In that sense, work is analogous to my favorite type of workout: boxing. Boxing is fast-paced and varied, and it exercises my whole body if I do it right. Some days my workout is light, as I hone my skills on the speed bag or by shadowboxing. On other days, I exhaust myself pounding on the heavy bag.

Work is a lot like that. Some days I make it look easy, applying my skills to achieve great results. Other days I go home feeling as if I have been run over by a bus. If I can remember, however, that work is my daily "workout," I can focus on building the skills God wants me to exercise wherever I am. On the job, we can practice leadership skills and learn compassion. We can explore and overcome weaknesses. We can take risks, get feedback, learn, and grow. Work is a gift of God, as long as we accept it a day at a time. Knowing this truth empowers us to approach our work with a more playful and open attitude.

While you are between jobs, remind yourself that the new position you find will not be the answer to all of your problems; it will be just another place to keep growing with God. If you are in a job but really need a change, focus on the skills you can hone right now. Make the most of your workout wherever you are.

One Small Step for Today

Many jobs out there are not dependent on a particular credential but on transferable skills and the ability to communicate those skills to others. Can you write well, speak persuasively, manage people, or complete a project on time and on budget? Employers need those skills. As you read position descriptions, don't focus solely on checking off the skills you already have. Look for where God may be inviting you to grow. Then start circling those skills in job ads. Like a good boxer, mix up your training and feel your muscles grow!

The Beauty of Failure

It is for freedom that Christ has set us free.
Stand firm, then, and do not let yourselves
be burdened again by a yoke of slavery.
—Galatians 5:1

I quit my first "real" job. After long months in a situation that was not a good fit for me, it simply became clear that God wanted me somewhere else. Reaching that point was tough. Even though I felt God was calling me to do it, leaving that job made me feel like a failure, especially since I had not been that great at what I was doing.

I like to be successful, and I'm sure you do too. Most of us want to be effective in our work, whether that means feeling confident about doing our best or building confidence in others by helping them do their best. We have expectations of ourselves, and we are aware of the expectations of others and don't want to disappoint. We want to be good stewards of the talents, education, and knowledge God has entrusted to us. We all want to hear "Well done," whether from family, employer, colleagues, friends, or the Lord Jesus himself.

Sometimes, however, that desire to succeed crosses the line into a fear of failure. That is dangerous ground. As Peter tells us, "people are slaves to whatever masters them" (2 Peter 2:19, NRSV). It is only a step from fear of failure to slavery to it. Too often the threat of "failure" on the job seems like a threat to everything good in our lives. If we are not judged successful, we fear losing the love of spouse, honor of children, and respect of our peers. Sure, we also worry about losing the job, losing our home, losing the lifestyle to which we have grown accustomed.

But we also fear losing our dignity, our sense of self-worth, and our professional or personal reputation.

One antidote for the fear of failure is to shift our focus from measuring success to accepting the many forms of beauty and goodness around us. We can rejoice at all the elements of our lives that do not depend on our vocational success.

Last night my wife and I had dinner alone and relished each other's company. I savored the aromas and tastes of the food as I cherished the time to talk and laugh without interruptions. Later I held my breath watching one of my children sleep, and then I listened to some of my favorite music before settling into a deep sleep. Each of these moments was a pleasure from the hand of God. They came with no striving or fear. They were not dependent on me making things happen on the job or on a job search.

God has surrounded us with amazing, guilt-free gifts that enrich every day if we would only stop striving for a moment and embrace them. The Lord wants us to enjoy these gifts, but we can't if we spend our days running in fear before the whip of success. Don't fear failure, and don't put too much emphasis on success; find the beauty and joy God has placed all around you.

One Small Step for Today

Take time each day—even if it is only a few minutes—to contemplate something beautiful. Lose yourself in an amazing book or your favorite music. Enjoy a sunset or go for a walk in the woods. Visit an art museum or a planetarium. Beauty shouts forth the existence of God and teaches us what God's heart is like. Thus beauty feeds our souls. Even (and especially) in the midst of the striving, worrying, and pushing for success that is inevitably part of the job search, beauty is the rain that turns our arid hearts into an oasis.

Building Bicycles

Whatever you do, whether in word or deed, do it all in the name of the Lord Jesus, giving thanks to God the Father through him. —Colossians 3:17

Orville and Wilbur Wright made their names by building a flying machine, but they made their living building bicycles. After starting a small printing business in the 1880s, the brothers bought their first bicycles in 1892 and soon became passionate about riding. They were known locally for both their cycling and mechanical skills, and many of their friends soon requested assistance with bicycle repair. The hobby became a trade in 1893 when they set up a bike repair and rental shop. Although they maintained some involvement in their printing work until 1899, they turned over most of the operations to a partner to pursue the bicycle business. In 1895 they began to manufacture their own bicycle line.

The Wrights' work with bicycles contributed greatly to their success with the first true airplane in 1903. In their production and repair work, they learned much about aerodynamics and wind resistance, as well as the chain and sprocket propulsion system they would adapt for their plane. Their bike shop also provided the brothers with the space and tools to refine their designs and the cash to fund them.*

Like the Wright brothers, where we start is not always where we will end up. In fact, it is rare these days to train for a particular career and then stay in one job or even one type of job for a

---

*"Who Were Wilbur and Orville?" Smithsonian Institute, National Air and Space Museum, www.nasm.si.edu/wrightbrothers/who/1895/biketoflight.cfm (accessed May 14, 2012).

lifetime. But we have not adjusted mentally to this reality. Many job seekers (including me at some points) get discouraged if they have to take a job for which they were not trained. Are you a recent graduate, forced to return to your parents' home because you are unable to launch the career you prepared for? Are you an experienced professional who has been laid off and can't find another position in your profession or at your old pay grade? It can be demoralizing to take a temporary job in an unrelated field or accept inferior wages. But this may be your bicycle shop.

Think about it: if the Wright brothers had not learned to build bicycles, they may never have built a plane. You never know why God has put a particular opportunity in front of you. That short-term job that seems beneath you may very well be the Lord's apprenticeship program. Ask God before you reject an opportunity because it doesn't pay enough or match your training. Where you begin is just a beginning. God can lay a foundation through unexpected work experiences. In that situation, learn everything you can, and ask God to help you make the most of your training. First learn to ride. Before you know it, you may be flying.

One Small Step for Today

If you are working in a job that is not a long-term match for you, focus on what skills it can give you that may prepare you for a better-fit job later. What skills are you using that you enjoy? Which skills do you wish you were using? Visit O-NET OnLine and try the advanced search tool called Skills Search (www.onetonline.org/skills). Check off the skills you would like to use in an employment setting and research jobs that fit those skills, including the preparation required. Then, as you build your skills, you can plan for the future.

State Your Purpose

My goal is that they may be encouraged in heart and united in love, so that they may have the full riches of complete understanding. —Colossians 2:2

Have you ever been watching a movie or reading a book when you suddenly realize that a particular character is you? Not literally, but the role that character is playing is you at your best moments. When you recognize yourself in a character, what do you see? What purpose does your character fulfill?

When I take a step back, I realize that all of my favorite stories have the same theme. In every one there is an unsuspecting hero and a wise mentor. The hero typically has a lot of potential but is a mess and doubts whether he or she has the right stuff to save the day. The insightful mentor, through patient teaching and well-placed challenges, develops the hero from rough wood into a well-honed tool for a righteous cause.

While I see some of myself in the reluctant hero, what I truly long to be is the mentor—the champion for the best in others. There is nothing I love more than helping people find their purpose. I see my task as helping others figure out what special function God has given them, develop that function to its potential, and learn to use it. That is what I believe the job search should be about for Christians.

God gives everything a purpose. You only have to think of the hundreds of prophecies that foretold the coming of Jesus to see that the Lord works intentionally, infusing all of life with meaning that unfolds only according to God's timetable. The Lord gave the first human beings a function (Genesis 1:28). Abraham became the father of nations. David was anointed shepherd-king for God's people. Esther was born to save her people from genocide. John the Baptist was the preparer of the Way. Paul was the apostle to the Gentiles. All of the friends of God are given a purpose—a function—to fulfill. Our smaller purpose can be used by God to accomplish a much greater divine purpose.

Imagine yourself as a tool—a hammer. What purpose do you fulfill? You pound nails, right? Now, the same hammer can pound nails to hang pictures or to build a house. As long as you are pounding nails, you are fulfilling the purpose for which you were designed. Imagine using a hammer for turning screws or swatting flies or painting a wall. What result do you get? A tool used for the wrong purpose is at best ineffective and at worst dangerous.

We each have been given a function to fulfill. We can perform that function in a variety of settings with excellence. God knows every construction project needs a hammer, and the Lord arranges for people with the right gift to be in the right spot when needed. Make yourself available to God, and ask the Spirit to make clear what job is yours to do. When you know your purpose, you can see much more clearly what positions could be right for you. Ask God to show you what nails need to be hammered.

One Small Step for Today

Want to clarify your purpose? Start with the list of characters from movies, books, and the Bible that most resonate with you. My list was quite varied, but all the stories shared one common theme. What is the common theme of your list? If you'd like more help, try the guided questionnaire I have designed called the PurposeFinder, available at www.aaronbasko.com.

Deal Breakers

Give your servant success today by granting him favor in the presence of this man.
—Nehemiah 1:11

One of my favorite leaders in Scripture is Nehemiah, the man who began to rebuild a broken-down Jerusalem. I especially admire how he took the lessons learned on his secular job, working for a pagan king, and put those lessons to work for God's people in their time of need. Nehemiah was a Jew in exile, serving in the court of the king of Persia, but he kept up with the news from back home. When he heard about the plight of Jerusalem and the remnant who had been left there, Nehemiah was moved by God—first to distress and then to action.

What Nehemiah wanted was to lead an expedition of laborers and supplies back to Jerusalem, there to begin the daunting task of rebuilding the Holy City. But Nehemiah was a servant (and by that, you can essentially read "slave") to the Persian king. Without the king's permission and financial support, the expedition would never happen.

Therefore, before making his request of the Persian king, Nehemiah got the attention of the King of heaven. And in both of his requests, Nehemiah asked specifically for what he needed: favor in the king's eyes and permission for the hazardous and expensive work project. You see, Nehemiah had learned on the job that laying his personal problems before the king could be hazardous to his health. But God answered his prayer, and the king granted his request.

Can you apply Nehemiah's leadership lessons to your job search? Imagine your next job interview as a kind of royal court. You are all too aware that you are the supplicant, the job seeker.

But you have a concern, an issue that requires favor from the one in authority. Maybe you wonder how family-friendly the company is. Maybe you have concerns about the amount of travel or the flexibility of the hours. Maybe you need a particular level of health insurance or wonder about education benefits. You want the job, but your ability to survive in the position depends on the answers to one or more key questions.

Don't be hesitant about asking for what you need—first of God and then of the "king." Jesus affirms that our Father knows what we need before we ask him (Matthew 6:8). The worst-case scenario is that God says no, but in that case, you can trust that the Lord has a better option in mind. Taking the request to God is also a way to discern whether the concern is a true need or a more superficial desire.

Once you have asked God, feel free to ask prospective employers. Do so respectfully, and I recommend that you wait until the end of the process, after you and the employer have determined that the job is a good fit. This shows that you are serious about the work and not just the benefits. If you have a "deal breaker," whether salary, benefits, or schedule, name it. Nehemiah teaches us to start off knowing what we need and to be willing to ask for it.

One Small Step for Today

When negotiating salary, remember these guidelines:

- Whenever possible allow the employer to bring up salary. If you are asked early in the process, say that salary is negotiable and that you want to confirm a good fit for the position first.
- Do not include personal expenses or circumstances in any negotiation.
- If the salary does not work for you, state what would work and ask if there is flexibility.
- Consider what other benefits might also be valuable to you in the equation.

Waiting for a New Name

Then the man said, "You shall no longer be called Jacob, but Israel, for you have striven with God and with humans, and have prevailed." —Genesis 32:28, NRSV

Struggle is a part of life that most of us would rather do without. When you are job hunting, that sense of struggle intensifies. You need to provide for yourself, and you may be fighting to pay bills, relocate, or pin down your career path. You keep forging ahead, even when you seem to be making little progress. As much as this struggle can wear a person down, it can also build true strength and determination.

Some of my peers had a lot of success in high school. Many won scholarships, and some went on to top colleges and universities. Most grew up in families that placed high value on education and sacrificed to provide their children with opportunities to achieve their lofty dreams. It was instructive to watch these friends as they entered the work world. Some fell into day-to-day lives that seem very different from the big dreams they had. Some seemed to wander aimlessly. Others were snatched up by wild adventures, but not always the kind their parents hoped to see. Many of us in this group probably felt like our early momentum—great grades, good schools, and strong families—should have carried us further.

The contrast to this, however, has been seeing other friends who had less "momentum" in high school. They did not necessarily have the highest scores or the most recognition. They did not attend big-name schools or win major scholarships, but now many of them seem more settled and focused than their peers. I believe the success of this second group can be found in their willingness to struggle and persevere. They knew they would have to get busy and make things happen. They did not, by and large, have delusions of grandeur to distract them. They selected niches, sized them up, and conquered—leaving some of us in the dust.

Perseverance is essential in both our Christian walk and the career search, and for Christians, the two should be tied together. Some of the most significant moments of my walk with God have followed directly those times that required the most perseverance. After a month or two of gritting my teeth and holding on to my faith with both hands, suddenly the Holy Spirit would breathe some fresh sense of God's presence into my life, and I would see clearly who I was and how I had grown. Like Jacob, at these times I have felt like I have been given a new name as I suddenly saw how God wanted me to step forward from that point.

I don't look forward to the times of struggle, but I have come to anticipate and value the new name and renewed sense of purpose enough that I appreciate them. Until the day your struggle is at an end, like Jacob, hold on until God blesses you with a clearer view of who you are called to become.

One Small Step for Today

When God changed Jacob's name, Jacob's destiny changed with it. Do you know what your name means? If not, find out. Ask God if your name is related to the purpose for which you were created. Revelation 2:17 says, "To everyone who conquers . . . I will give a white stone, and on the white stone is written a new name that no one knows except the one who receives it" (NRSV). Let your imagination run wild with that for a moment. What name would you hope you would receive from Christ? What does that tell you about how you should spend your working hours?

Use the Yardstick

*For this reason I remind you to fan
into flame the gift of God, which is in
you through the laying on of my hands.*
—2 Timothy 1:6

My sister is a great example of someone who knows what God
has gifted her to do and has used that knowledge as a litmus test
for career decision. She has always been amazing with children.
Even when she was a teen, she would walk into a room and all
the kids would be pulled toward her by a force as strong as a trac-
tor beam from the mother ship. There was something about the
way God built her that made children understand that she could
be trusted with their secrets and their hearts.

As time went on, she explored and developed this gift, and
it became clear that her true glory and purpose were in serving
children with special circumstances. While some of her friends
gravitated toward the classroom, she seemed to be always drawn
to one-on-one work with those with physical or developmental
issues. It has not always been an easy path. She has had to work
hard to define her niche. When she has described her work with
terminally ill children in a hospital or in an orphanage in Haiti, I
have thought to myself, "Wow, I can't imagine doing that. That is
God's purpose shining through."

As she has grown professionally and personally, my sister has
adjusted her focus a few times—from families, to hospitals, to
teaching organizations. She returned to school for a graduate degree in social work, which shifted her focus again. While each
environment has had its shortcomings, I have seen her find joy
and value in each because her special purpose—the gift God has

given her—to impact the lives of needy children has not changed. This has been her constant yardstick. At each decision point, she has been able to ask, "Will this allow me to better focus on what I love to do?"

If you are offered a job tomorrow, how will you decide if it is a match for you? What is your yardstick—the measure against which you will evaluate your career choices five, ten, or twenty years from now? That yardstick is an understanding of the gift that God has given you. Keep it closeby and assess your choices against it periodically. How is your life measuring up to God's specifications?

One Small Step for Today

God's special gifting often appears in our earliest years. You'll often hear stories about the doctor who put bandages on stuffed animals when she was little, or the actor who by the age of five already knew how to entertain even the toughest room. Ask your parents or others who knew you well as a child to tell you some stories. What was it that surprised or impressed them about you even at a young age? What has been the consistent theme of your interest and activities? This is a fun and insightful way to look for God's fingerprint on your life.

Going Downhill Fast

*Work willingly at whatever you
do, as though you were working
for the Lord rather than for people.*
—Colossians 3:23, NLT

The Lord blessed me with a great father, but I have also learned a tremendous amount from my father-in-law. From him I have learned a lot about houses and cars, plumbing and electric. He has taught me how to hunt and how to take care of things I want to last a long time. He has also taught me quite a bit about work.

One of my father-in-law's lessons is that you have to have an outlet, some activity that you are passionate about other than your job. For him, it is mountain biking. Dad, now retired and in his midsixties, is a competitive biker who can ride circles around guys thirty years his junior. Two or three times a week, in all weather, he drives to the trails to bike. He has broken his collarbone three times coming down steep West Virginia hillsides. He has also spent countless hours in trail maintenance, race officiating, and bike repair. An International Mountain Bicycling Association bumper sticker on his car declares, "Long Live Long Rides."

My father-in-law's dedication to biking has helped him maintain some sense of balance in life. I have learned from him that work is not everything, nor should it be the only thing that receives your passion and energy. Jobs will come and go during your life. Through all these changing circumstances, God is working on that which is permanent—you, becoming more like Jesus, bringing more light, more goodness, and more excellence into all areas where you can make an impact—home, work, church, and community.

Practice this sense of balance and perspective in your job search. While I'm not suggesting you spend every day mountain biking instead of job searching, why not volunteer, find a hobby, invest in your family, develop strong friendships, and read great books? Chances are at some point in your career you will need these things to keep you grounded.

Paul says, "Whatever you do, work at it with all your heart" (Colossians 3:23). Getting the right job will not make you the kind of person God created you to be. You will just be the employed version of you. Working with all your heart at whatever the Lord puts in the reach of your hands is your opportunity to build on the foundation God wants to lay in your life.

Now that Dad is retired, his church has realized what great skills he has. It seems like he is involved in every project that needs leadership and energy. Maybe he'll shift more of his biking passion to service, but I think it's just as likely he'll still be screaming down the hills when he's eighty. After all, he still has one good collarbone left.

One Small Step for Today

Take a look at a job stress list such as CareerCast's "Most Stressful Jobs" or CNN Money's "Stressful Jobs that Pay Badly."* If your target job (or one like it) is listed here, take note of the major stressors are and consider how you will cope with them. Use this time to learn good stress management habits. Practice making time *now* for things that help you recharge and stay healthy. These habits will be more likely to stick with you when you land that great position.

*See Victoria Brienza, "The 10 Most Stressful Jobs of 2012," CareerCast, www.careercast.com/jobs-rated/10-most-stressful-jobs-2012 (accessed May 14, 2012); Jessica Dickler, "Stressful Jobs That Pay Badly," Money, money.cnn.com/galleries/2009/pf/0910/gallery.stressful_jobs/index.html (accessed May 14, 2012).

Be Present to God

Better is one day in your courts than a thousand elsewhere. —Psalm 84:10

You could turn to the Lord now for help during your job search, only to forget and grow distant from God once you find the job you seek. This is what Israel did after the Lord brought them into the Promised Land. God can use this time of your job search to deepen your faith if you ask the Holy Spirit to be present in this experience with you. But you will lose all the benefit from this time if you do not continue to invite God's constant presence as you move into your work. Your job search is such an immensely valuable time because you can build now the patterns that will serve you well for the rest of your working life.

What was the highest compliment that the Old Testament paid to the heroes of the faith? They walked with God. Enoch, Abraham, Moses, and Elijah are not honored for their sterling character or perfect track records; they are honored for their fellowship with God. They had a constant, ongoing relationship with the living God. Remarkable!

In fact, God's presence is the source of all good in our lives. It is God's presence that separates a life of significance from a life devoid of any meaning. Without the Lord's presence, there is no warmth, no light, and no hope. Christ rescued us so that we could enjoy his presence and so that his very life would live within us. The miracle of Christianity is friendship with the Creator of the universe.

Make the most of that relationship. Invite God into each thing you do. Praise the Lord on every occasion you can. Talk to God. When you go into an interview or meeting, take God with you. When you research or prepare, let the Lord guide you. Enjoy Jesus' friendship and his presence every moment you can get. You will find perspective in difficult challenges, peace that makes no sense, and joy in things that before seemed too small to notice.

Best of all, you will begin to have a sense for how your fellowship with God transforms your relationships with others—with coworkers and customers, with managers and vendors. Your relationship with the Lord will be manifest in how you relate to your environment as well, whether it is through better stewardship of human and natural resources or through sensitivity to God's power and presence in every context and situation. Enjoy God's fellowship in all you say and do, wherever you are and wherever you go.

One Small Step for Today

Invite God into your new position in advance—now, before you even know what the job will be. Envision what your working environment might look like, and purposefully ask Christ to make it his position, not yours. See yourself in different activities that might be a part of your work, such as speaking with coworkers, taking part in a meeting, interacting with customers or clients, working alone. In each situation you can think of, ask God to go with you, to be present in a tangible way, and to be glorified in all you say and do. Invite God now to continue building your relationship when you move from the job hunt to the job itself.

Our Daily Fruit

Taste and see that the LORD *is good;*
blessed is the one who takes refuge in him.
—Psalm 34:8

In the book *Perelandra,* which is part of C. S. Lewis's classic space trilogy, the central character, Elwin Ransom, travels to the lush planet of Perelandra and is awed by the beauty and richness of a golden world of floating islands and frolicking miniature dragons. In many ways, his experiences there offer a parallel to the biblical account of Eden and the Fall.

Throughout his adventures, Ransom feeds himself on the fantastic variety of exquisite fruit found everywhere in Perelandra. He discovers one type of fruit is even more delectable than the standard variety. Initially tempted to search only for this kind and discard the others, Ransom begins to recognize that a right spiritual attitude is reflected in the acceptance of what is given, while the reverse—coveting one type of thing over what is offered—is the root of much human evil. Ransom discusses this with Lady Mother, Perelandra's version of Eve, as an analogy for how humans wander from accepting God's will:

> One goes into the forest to pick food and already the thought of one fruit rather than another has grown up in one's mind. Then, it may be, one finds a different fruit and not the fruit one thought of. One joy was expected and another is given. But this I had never noticed before—that the very moment of the finding there is in the mind a kind of thrusting back, or setting aside. The picture of the fruit you have *not* found is still, for a moment, before you. And if you wished—if it were possible to wish—you could keep it there. You could send your soul after the good you had expected,

instead of turning to the good you had got. You could refuse the real good; you could make the real fruit taste insipid by thinking of the other.*

For a job seeker, the temptation to refuse "real good" in favor of coveting something else is a big challenge. How can we help but focus on the better security, income, and sense of purpose sure to come with finally landing that elusive ideal job? In my own job search, it seemed like everything good was just out of reach, and yet God was surrounding me with fantastic, accessible fruit. During that season of time, my wife and I learned how to support and protect each other. We grew closer to and came to depend on our families. I also never would have started this book—another unexpected blessing.

We always have a choice: we can taste the unknown joys that roll toward us, or we can starve ourselves by clinging to the images we create in our heads. Eat the fruit that God is giving you today. "Everything God created is good, and nothing is to be rejected if it is received with thanksgiving" (1 Timothy 4:4).

One Small Step for Today

When seeking "the perfect job," getting a realistic view of the goal is difficult. Take advantage of data-driven Internet resources to build an objective profile of your target positions, such as the Occupational Outlook Handbook (www.bls.gov/oco) by the Bureau of Labor Statistics or the Department of Labor's Career One Stop (www.acinet.org). Explore statistics about working conditions, salary, job outlook, and qualifications before pursuing a position further.

*C. S. Lewis, *Perelandra* (New York: Scribner, 1972), 59.

A Certain Friendship

*I do not call you servants any longer,
because the servant does not know what
the master is doing; but I have called you
friends, because I have made known to
you everything that I have heard from
my Father.* —John 15:15, NRSV

As far as I can tell, the disciples offered Jesus only two things: earnestness and friendship. I like the way the movie *The Gospel of John* presents the disciples. As Jesus introduces himself to each of them and as they spread the word to one another, it is clear that they have been searching. Their eyes flash in expectation as one tells another, "We've found the one we've been looking for!" Here is the first kernel of faith.*

The disciples are earnest in their desire to find the Messiah, and they obviously have been conversing about it. They know which friends to go to right away. John and Andrew follow John the Baptist until he points them to Jesus as the Christ. Andrew runs to get his brother Simon. Phillip finds his buddy Nathanael, who has been seeking God's face under a fig tree. Their hearts are ready, and it takes only a brief conversation with Jesus to ignite the tinder into flame.

The disciples also offered Jesus their friendship. Jesus certainly encountered great highs and lows in his ministry. Both are better shared with companions. Jesus' choices for his inner circle do not appear to be based on who was most capable, but perhaps he selected the ones who most wanted to be with him. These were the

---

*The Gospel of John, directed by Philip Saville, Toronto: Visual Bible International, 2003.

ones who were "all in." They didn't always understand his teaching, but they loved him, trusted him, and wanted to be with him.

We can learn a lot from the disciples. Can we offer Jesus our earnest expectation that he will show up daily to meet with us? Does it take only a fresh word from the Lord for us to jump in with both feet? Do we offer him our deepest friendship or just our dutiful obedience? Being with Jesus should matter more than knowing exactly where he is taking us in our lives.

In the job search, most of us have no idea where we will end up, and we aren't likely to know until we reach our ultimate destination. This is true most of the time in our lives, but during the job search it may be a little more acceptable to admit it. If you can recognize now that you don't know where your path is leading but that everything is okay because you are walking it with Jesus, you will have learned a truth that will serve you all your life. Friendship with the Lord is worth far more than the ability to see a few steps into the future.

The disciple's joy was made complete when the resurrected Jesus kept his promise to meet them in Galilee. But I believe his most important promise to them is also his promise to us: that he will be with us always, to the end of the age. With that promise, Jesus allows all of his disciples to live out our earnest friendship with him for the rest of our lives.

One Small Step for Today

Commitment to Jesus but flexibility in where he leads you can be a powerful combination. Don't narrow your search too much. Brainstorm a wide variety of fields where you can use your skills and then learn more about them. Keep your résumé flexible by replacing an objective statement ("to secure a position in X with an industry-leading company") with a profile statement ("experienced professional with proven ability to X, Y, and Z"). This focuses on what you can offer, helping employers see you as the solution to their problem.

Give Me a Push

*My child, do not regard lightly the
discipline of the Lord, or lose heart
when you are punished by him; for
the Lord disciplines those whom he
loves, and chastises every child whom
he accepts.* —Hebrews 12:5-6, NRSV

My friend and colleague Charlie has a fantastic story of God's intervening in his life to change its direction. One day I asked him how he decided that career services was the right fit for him. With a twinkle in his eye, he said, "You want to hear the whole story?"

Charlie started college, but after marriage, he dropped out and worked in a coal mine for the next sixteen years. Eventually his wife convinced him to finish his degree, but he never expected to use it. "[Coal mining] was all I knew," he told me. "I hadn't really seen anything else. I probably would have stayed in the mines for thirty years if God hadn't given me a push."

That push came in the form of a layoff. Suddenly Charlie realized he had no real plan. "I went to see the career services director at the college where I had finished my degree and said, 'You have to help me!' I met with him ten times."

Charlie did get help, but the career services director also pointed him toward an opening as an admissions representative at the college. "Can you imagine what my application must have looked like? I was a thirty-eight-year-old miner with absolutely no experience in any area of higher education. My résumé basically consisted of the different types of equipment I knew how to use. I can only think that my contact in career services helped me get it."

Charlie was a hardworking admissions representative who moved up to interim director when his boss had to take a leave of absence. Soon the director of career services position opened up. He has been counseling students in their career planning ever since. "I look back and say, 'How did I ever get here?'" he admits. "But sometimes God has to extract you from where you feel comfortable."

There are times in life when we get comfortable where we are. We become inflexible and lose our sensitivity to God's movements. In those cases, the Lord may need to pry us out of our hiding spots. It can be an unnerving and painful experience. It may be tempting to become bitter or to blame the people God uses to force us in another direction. But God allows a jarring experience to move us out where the Spirit can guide us forward.

You may be in a job hunt precisely because you've been "extracted." God has allowed an unwelcome push to tell you it is time to move on to the next part of your journey. Don't resent the change. This is for God's glory and your good, so use this time to regain your flexibility and sensitivity to God's will. Be pliable in God's hands and watch the Master at work moving you to places you never would have expected.

One Small Step for Today

Networking is building and investing in relationships that can help you identify job opportunities, such as Charlie's relationship with the career services director. Who do you already know who has connections in your desired field—friends and family, former teachers or coaches, your doctor or mail carrier? When they ask how you are doing, let them know you have been hard at work on your job search. Ask if they have any advice or if they know anyone who could help you. The more people you know, the more likely you are to be connected with someone who can point you in the right direction.

Courage to Obey

> *Have I not commanded you? Be strong*
> *and courageous. Do not be afraid; do*
> *not be discouraged, for the* LORD *your*
> *God will be with you wherever you go.*
> —Joshua 1:9

One of the best examples of quiet courage and determination in the Bible is Joshua. He started out as Moses' assistant (Deuteronomy 1:38); was one of only two spies who returned from scouting out the land of Canaan with an optimistic report (Numbers 14:8-9); and after Moses' death, became leader of the Israelites and marched them into the Promised Land (Joshua 1:1-9). God's words when Joshua took command became the theme of his life—dual themes in fact: to be obedient and to be strong and courageous.

Obedience is an important quality in a leader. We want our leaders to understand what it means to take orders as well as to give them. Joshua was crystal clear about that, for he had assisted Moses for years and implemented his leader's instructions. Apparently Joshua also understood that Moses' commands had actually been God's, because when Moses was gone, Joshua just transferred his obedience to the Lord.

One of the first commands God gave Joshua captures the second theme: to be strong and courageous. It is a refrain Joshua heard from the Lord repeatedly. He heard it in Deuteronomy 31 when Moses established Joshua as his successor, and in Joshua 1 the Lord proclaimed it four times in just eighteen verses. Later, in chapter 10, Joshua passed along the command to his men. Over and over again, Joshua's life proclaimed, "Don't be afraid. Take courage."

And Joshua seemed to take his courage from following God's commands. As a young man, he discounted the fact that the Israelites looked like grasshoppers compared with the Canaanites (as the other spies reported), because God had told them they could take the land. Years later, when Joshua was the one in charge and facing the fortifications of Jericho, he didn't blink when God told him to launch an attack with nothing but trumpets. He followed God's instructions to the letter, requiring the people to march on the exact number of days and the exact number of times around the city—in silence or shouting, precisely as the Lord commanded.

Most of the Israelites must have thought their leader had gone crazy! But Joshua was effective in his leadership because the people obeyed him. Maybe they gained courage by observing his confidence in what obedience to God could accomplish. Indeed, Joshua's life seems to indicate that obedience can be a source of courage—and success. Joshua's obedience in the past had led to his position of leadership. God made it clear that continued obedience would have similar results: "Be careful to obey all the law my servant Moses gave you; do not turn from it to the right or the left, that you may be successful wherever you go" (Joshua 1:7).

As you seek to be obedient to God's purpose and plan, remember the Lord's command to Joshua to be bold. And keep in mind that through your obedience to God's will, you may be strengthened, taking courage in knowing that you are walking in the way God has called you.

One Small Step for Today

What about the job search provokes the most anxiety or fear in you? Preparing a cover letter and résumé or promoting yourself through networking? Doing job research or being interviewed? The job search forces most of us outside our comfort zone eventually, but like Joshua, we are called to be courageous in all situations. Whatever your biggest challenge may be, give God the chance to come through for you.

Showdown

For I am with you, and no one is going to attack and harm you, because I have many people in this city. —Acts 18:10

All job seekers face the burdens of self-doubt and insecurity; even the new college graduate wonders what the future holds and how she or he is going to face it. In a difficult economy, desperation adds an edge to the uncertainty. But to those universal challenges that obstruct the road ahead, the mature job seeker adds the load of family responsibilities, a thirty-year mortgage, a car payment, and shrinking retirement funds, which crowd around like gunslingers at the O.K. Corral.

For the job changer, the question is, "Do I jump into the churning sea, or do I try to patch up a dilapidated raft?" The risk is bigger when you have invested years in your current position or field. It is more common for job changers to have families or other responsibilities that will have to jump with them.

Job changers are also often more subject to criticism than first-time seekers, even from friends and family. Someone always seems to ask, "Isn't that a big risk to take with a family to support? Besides, don't you already have a job that pays the bills? And what about all those years of studying for this career?"

If God is leading you toward something else, you'll want to have an answer ready for those who question you. This will keep discouragement away and keep you connected to what God is showing you day by day. Some people make critical comments because they would not have the courage to jump from their own rafts. Instead of pointing this out, however, be quietly confident and remind them that you already trust God for the big things—

your life and well-being. Surely you can trust the Lord with your work as well.

In job change situations, sometimes just knowing that you are doing the right thing is the hardest part. Start with prayer. But you should also ask God to send backup. Mature job changers often feel that they are alone—that they are the only ones taking this kind of risk and that no one understands. That's why part of your prayer should be that God would send you reinforcements. A couple of good friends or professional contacts who are praying for your success can make a huge difference. When the gunslingers start to circle, it helps to have a posse at your back.

Well before I arrived at my current job, the Lord had already been preparing the path. Not only had God clearly guided me along the way, but I found out later that two of the staff members in my office had asked their Bible study group to pray for nearly nine months that God would bring the right person into my position. God answered their prayers.

They saw me as the answer to that prayer. Ask God which of these contacts you should ask to guard your back. Critics are easy to find, but whom can you reach out to who will stand behind you in prayer and ride with you in tough terrain? When your doubts circle you, ask God to call in the reinforcements.

One Small Step for Today

Prayer is like the plow that turns over the hard earth and creates deep furrows in the ground so that seeds will take root instead of just blowing away. Make a list of the people you can count on to pray for you until God opens the right door. Ask them to pray for you until you find a position. You want all the backup you can get.

Proceed with Confidence

*When they saw the courage of Peter
and John and realized that they were
unschooled, ordinary men, they were
astonished and they took note that these
men had been with Jesus.* —Acts 4:13

As I coach people in their career planning and make hires as a manager, I see what a big role confidence plays in getting the job. I'm not talking about swagger, although there are some jobs where that is a fit. I'm referring to the assurance that comes from knowing who you are, what abilities you can offer, and why you want this job.

Every year, I have been called on to help bright, talented students who flounder when they hit their first job fair or interview. The feedback I receive about them is that managers like them but feel they have no gravitas, no focus, and no drive. I have seen the same in candidates whose answers meander all over the place. Maybe this is a career change for them, so I don't expect them to know every detail about the position. But too often, instead of convincing me that they are right for the job, they sound like they are trying to convince themselves.

That's part of why I like Acts 4:13. Peter and John are new to religious persecution; they have never been called to face the priests before. They don't have a script or a manual to follow; they don't know what response will inspire which consequences or how their civil disobedience will be viewed by their peers in the young Christian community. So, they don't know *what* they are doing, but they do know *why* they are doing it. As a result, when interviewed they don't stutter or second-guess themselves. Even though they are only learning what this particular job entails, they are committed to following their purpose.

The religious authorities learn their secret: "these men had been with Jesus." The same strength of purpose the priests and Levites had seen in the face and actions of Jesus when he cleared the temple or challenged them with his teaching (see John 5:19-47) was now evident in these former fishermen. They were bold and confident because they had spent time with Jesus the Christ.

That is where your boldness should come from as well. If you spend time with Jesus, you gain the right perspective about your work and about particular job hunt experiences. There is no need to fear an interview or its outcome, because you know that the Lord is sovereign over it. There is also no reason for false humility. You know why you were created (to glorify God and to serve according to the gifts you have been given). You know the Lord has a plan for you (Jeremiah 29:11). You know that God can open or close a particular door for you based on what is in your eternal best interest. It is time to be bold! Demonstrate a desire to make a difference and to let some of God's glory shine through you. Show people you have been with Jesus.

One Small Step for Today

When you know who you are (and whose you are!) you can approach pressure situations with courage and confidence. Start by eliminating second-guessing from your speech—those qualifying or pause-filling phrases such as "like," "just," "I guess," "maybe," and the dreaded "um." These undercut your credibility and take the power out of what you are saying. Instead of "um" or "like," pause slightly and catch your breath. Make your language as precise as possible, using numbers and clear examples. Tightening your language is a great way to display the confidence you have that God has equipped you to take on any challenge.

Office Manager

> *You have been faithful with a few things;*
> *I will put you in charge of many things.*
> *Come and share your master's happiness!*
> —Matthew 25:23

In an office setting, you typically come in contact with that indispensable employee, the office manager. The best office manager cares deeply about the success of the department more than for personal recognition or power. The office manager is good with details, careful with company resources, and fiercely loyal to a good leader. Some people in this role are stern, others jovial, and others quiet, but each one is a good steward, entrusted with people and supplies that are someone else's, and ready to give a true account at any moment.

As Christians, we are probably familiar with the concept of stewardship, most often in the context of using our money and talents to serve God. In Matthew 24:45, Jesus asks, "Who then is the faithful and wise servant, whom the master has put in charge of the servants in his household to give them their food at the proper time?" Aren't our jobs also gifts that God has entrusted into our care? Whether we manage people or tasks, others depend on us to do our jobs with excellence. We each have a sphere of influence, whether small or large, and we are accountable for the work we do. Ultimately, though, the people and resources that we influence do not belong to us, or even to the company, but have been entrusted to us by God.

In his masterful book *The Pursuit of God*, pastor and author A. W. Tozer asserted, "It is not what a man does that determines whether his work is sacred or secular, it is why he does it."* After reading that, I saw the goal of my job search differently. I began to pray earnestly for a position where I could find fulfillment using the gifts God had given me but where the position would not primarily be about me. I prayed, "Lord, where do *you* want to work? You pick the position, and I will represent you there. Make me your office manager. Show me what you want me to steward for you."

This change in mind-set transformed my experience. We need reminders that the job search process is not primarily about us; it is about God's plan in the world and our part in it. Regardless of the job title we seek or attain, each of us is an office manager, shepherding what God has put into our care but giving God all of the credit.

This lesson was one more blessing emerging from my job search. Since then, the Lord has given me the opportunity to be a steward in each position I've had. I am accountable to God for the way I do my work and for how I influence the lives around me. When I act as the Lord's office manager, it is for God's glory, my good, and the good of all those who work with me.

One Small Step for Today

Although employers may not use the word *stewardship*, companies want good stewards too. They want to be able to trust the people they hire with everything from people to paper clips. As you craft your résumé, include any experiences you have had in managing resources and relationships. Populate your résumé with action words that demonstrate the impact you have had. (Search online using the key words "résumé action words" to find sample lists.) Begin phrases with these action words to illustrate the type of stewardship an employer can expect from you.

---

*A. W. Tozer, *The Pursuit of God*. Tozer Legacy ed. (Camp Hill, Pa.: Christian Publications, 1982), 127.

This Means War

*By the sweat of your brow you will eat
your food until you return to the ground,
since from it you were taken; for dust
you are and to dust you will return.*
—Genesis 3:19

My imagination was captured recently reading the story of Douglas Bader, a British pilot in World War II. Bader joined the Royal Air Force (RAF) in 1930, but he lost part of both of his legs in a horrific crash in 1931. Against all predictions, Bader learned to walk again using artificial legs. When WWII broke out, Bader attempted to reenlist as a fighter pilot. Although he was initially refused, he persisted and became a squadron commander.

Not only was Bader one of the most successful fighter pilots in RAF history, but he helped create new tactics that changed the balance in the air war. In 1941 he was involved in a midair collision, which he barely survived, and ended up in a German POW camp. Among the POWs it was understood that the more Germans they could keep busy trying to track down escapees, the fewer soldiers would be available to fight the Allied forces. Bader himself tried to escape so many times that his captors took his legs from him. He finally received his freedom in 1945 when American forces liberated Colditz Castle, where he was being held.* Bader was determined to make an impact, whatever the obstacles, whatever the situation. Neither his physical disability nor his imprisonment kept him from bringing his best to the battle.

*Conn Iggulden and Hal Iggulden, *The Dangerous Book for Boys* (New York: HarperCollins, 2007), 205–6.

When God created human beings, work was part of the goodness of creation (Genesis 1:26-31), a gift of God bestowed on humankind. Of course, the twin gifts of dominion and stewardship encompass responsibilities as well as privileges, but in the beginning, there was greater balance in the relationship between those responsibilities and privileges. It was only after Adam and Eve fell from grace—by taking what had *not* been entrusted to them—that their relationship with work became toilsome.

Few people in our industrialized nation fully appreciate the agricultural toil described in Genesis 3:17-19. But we have our own experiences with toil as we labor to provide for ourselves and our loved ones. Some of the toil is connected with long hours, low wages, harsh working conditions, and unjust employers. Some toil emerges from difficult relationships with coworkers, clients, or customers. Some workplaces directly challenge Christian beliefs and values; others place people in ethical dilemmas that force difficult decisions and risk job security.

Here's the good news: Christ's redemptive work reverses the effects of the Fall, restoring the balance in relationships between men and women, human beings and creation, and humanity and our work in the world. Seize every opportunity—as you labor at the job search and as you work in whatever capacities God provides—to advance Christ's work in the world.

One Small Step for Today

Douglas Bader's story teaches us to look for opportunities to make maximum impact. To do this effectively, you must have a vision for what that impact looks like for you. In your vocation or in your sphere of influence, what fruit can you cultivate? What relationships can you restore to balance? What toil can you transform into well-earned rest? Then consider the steps you can take today to help you start having that kind of impact.

Dress for Success

Therefore, as God's chosen people, holy and dearly loved, clothe yourselves with compassion, kindness, humility, gentleness and patience. —Colossians 3:12

As an employer, I'm always shocked when a candidate shows up at an interview casually dressed. I realize that our culture is less formal than it was even a decade ago, but the job interview is a place for your very best. Casual dress can send signals that you lack professional experience and knowledge of what is expected in the workplace, especially if you are a less-experienced applicant. I have taken a candidate's dress into consideration, consciously or subconsciously, in my hiring decisions.

The idea of dressing for success carries over into the way we clothe ourselves spiritually. The Bible is very clear that our outward actions reflect the condition of our hearts. A job search can be a stressful time, which means that we can choose to be cranky, short with others, and self-absorbed, or we can decide to exhibit "compassion, kindness, humility, gentleness and patience." Although we may not realize it, those around us pick up on these traits almost as readily as they see our appearance.

One year I was interviewing candidates for a position in my office. The candidate pool was very strong, and I had some excellent choices, all of whom I felt would make a real contribution to the team. In the end, I chose an internal candidate, one with less experience on paper, but one whose character had truly impressed me. Evaluation after evaluation of his work from our team came back saying the same thing—humble, hard-working, team-oriented, a person of character. Even through difficult challenges in our office he had demonstrated consistency and perseverance. I realized that this person was the "best dressed" for the position.

You wear your faith just as surely as you wear your best interview clothes. As you meet those inevitable daily challenges, will what you wear be your best, for God's glory?

One Small Step for Today

Review a few websites that offer advice about dressing for an interview. Then start to build your interview outfit. (If you lack a professional wardrobe and can't afford to shop for one, check out DressforSuccess.org or CareerGear.com for gently used suits that are donated to meet such a need.) I recommend selecting two outfits in case of a last-minute spill or wardrobe malfunction. Prepare an emergency kit of other things you might need (umbrella, grooming items, spare tie or pantyhose, extra résumés and reference lists). God cares most about what is within, but you can reflect the Lord's excellence by making your outside match what God is creating on the inside.

Help Wanted: Famine Specialist

So Pharaoh asked them, "Can we find anyone like this man, one in whom is the spirit of God?" —Genesis 41:38

While studying two of my favorite figures in the Bible, Joseph and Daniel, I was struck by the similarities in their success stories. Both were dragged off from their homes under bad circumstances. Both achieved positions of great power within foreign governments—in part because both of them nailed their interview with a king! Most of all, Joseph and Daniel were able to bring God's power and presence to bear on their secular work. Let's consider Joseph first.

Throughout his life, Joseph was not a person who was afraid to say what he thought or believed. He was always ready to point to the reason for his confidence. I believe that even while a servant in Potiphar's house (Genesis 39:1-6), Joseph could not keep from mentioning that God was watching out for him. All the time, he must have remembered what God had promised in his childhood dreams. My guess is that when Potiphar noted his success and asked about it, Joseph pointed to the Lord in one way or another.

If you think I'm reading into the text too much, read further in Genesis 39. When Potiphar's wife is trying to draw Joseph in, he responds, "My master has withheld nothing from me except you, because you are his wife. How then could I do such a wicked thing and sin against God?" (verse 9). Joseph is confident he is doing the right things because he is sure of God's perspective.

Other people will cause you problems, as Potiphar's wife did for Joseph, but if you invite God with you in all circumstances, the Lord will work for your good. After the failed seduction, Joseph ended up falsely accused and imprisoned, but "the LORD was with him" and he practically became part of the prison staff (Genesis 39:21-23). God maneuvered Joseph into a position to accomplish a great purpose. When Pharaoh's two servants found themselves in jail too, God troubled their dreams and pointed them to Joseph.

After hearing about their dreams, Joseph assured his fellow prisoners that "interpretations belong to God" (Genesis 40:8). Having honored the Lord with this credit, Joseph was honored by God, first by discerning a correct interpretation (40:20-22) and later with an audience before Pharaoh (see Genesis 41). Once again Joseph brought God into the interview, telling Pharaoh, "God will give Pharaoh the answer he desires" (41:16). God ultimately honored Joseph by making him second in command over the whole nation of Egypt (41:37-45).

Joseph was successful because he knew that the Lord could give him a more effective letter of reference than he could give himself. Joseph invited God into his work, introduced the Lord to all his bosses, and the Lord lifted him up. Invite God into every step of your search process, and then invite the Lord into your work too.

One Small Step for Today

Someone has said that people may join organizations, but they leave bosses. While this isn't always the case, your boss will wield a lot of influence over your job satisfaction and effectiveness. Pray for your future boss today. Pray that you may work well with your boss and that this key relationship will allow you to have influence for good and for God in your new location. Pray that the Lord will give you wisdom in what to look for in a leader, and write down what qualities you think your ideal boss would have.

Help Wanted: Lion Tamer

> *The king talked with them, and he found none equal to Daniel, Hananiah, Mishael, and Azariah; so they entered the king's service.* —Daniel 1:19

Like Joseph, Daniel followed an amazing career path, experiencing extraordinary success but also extraordinary challenges. Daniel became God's missionary to the kings of Babylon and Persia. As rulers changed, he had a series of royal interviews that tested his value to the incoming ruler. Each time, Daniel pointed the king toward the Most High God, and each time the Lord defended Daniel against his enemies and lifted Daniel to a place of great influence.

As Jews living in forced exile, Daniel and his friends certainly faced temptations to turn away from God. They were deprived of family and homeland. Their captors changed their Hebrew names for others that honored the gods of Babylon, instructed the young men in a foreign culture, and even tried to change their diet. In every possible way, the captives were pushed to assimilate. Daniel and his friends adapted very successfully to most of the cultural norms, but they did not surrender their devotion to God.

Daniel negotiated with the chief official to receive a diet that would not break Jewish religious laws. The fact that Daniel chose food as his point of resistance is less important than what it represented: Daniel's resolve to honor God in his life. By his actions, Daniel offered himself in order that the Lord might work through him. Daniel chose allegiance to the God of Israel over any new authority or ruler in his life. (Notice that part of Daniel's strength undoubtedly came from the commitment he had made to his friends. This is the kind of accountability and support we need in our life of faith and work.)

God honored the choices of these four friends. When the chief official examined them after ten days on their new diet, Daniel and his friends were in excellent shape. When the king tested them at the end of their training, "he found them ten times better" than their peers or any of the reigning experts (Daniel 1:20). Their first interview was a success because they had already established their commitment to God's law and leading.

This pattern of success continued throughout Daniel's life, whether the crisis was a king's nightmare, a den of lions, or phantom writing on a wall. Daniel brought God's name before the royal court again and again. And by his presence in that place, Daniel provided a tangible reminder of God's power and an invitation to know the Lord.

As workers who are also disciples of Christ, we are all given a mission field—a place or a group of people within our sphere of influence. Invite God into your work, just as Daniel did. Daniel's example suggests that the best time to make that invitation is before you start—before the first interview. Trust the Lord with your career path, and be available to accomplish God's purpose. It is through you that God will be revealed to those who need the Lord most.

One Small Step for Today

Commit each opportunity to God before you pursue it, and at each stage of the process (application, interview, evaluation of a job offer), recommit. As much as you may think a particular opportunity must be the right one, discipline yourself to yield it to God. Follow Daniel's example and get some friends that can help you stay committed to the Lord's best. Remember that the Lord has promised to be with us, even in a strange land or in challenging circumstances—and the job search is both!

Get Ready to Shout

Some of the Pharisees in the crowd said to Jesus, "Teacher, rebuke your disciples!" "I tell you," he replied, "if they keep quiet, the stones will cry out." —Luke 19:39-40

Several years ago, I went on a mission trip to the Dominican Republic. The Dominicans I met were wonderful and warm and had a smile ready at any moment. The Christian brothers and sisters especially seemed to carry around a barely suppressed joy—and they did so in the face of poverty and hardship that most of us would find debilitating or outright paralyzing. One pastor would greet his congregation with, "The Lord bless you," and the whole room would shout back, "Amen!" Any small event could inspire this joy to burst forth.

Bill, one of the leaders of the organization we worked with, seemed to have internalized this explosive joy that was all around us. When we accomplished a project, he would provide a resounding "Hallelujah!" But he would belt out that same "Hallelujah!" whenever an obstacle had presented itself, and I would think, *What is that all about?* Was he viewing the problem from a more heavenly perspective—envisioning our hard work as a struggle against evil? Or was he perhaps thinking of how God would choose to prevail?

Eventually I realized that Bill was not rationalizing the present or anticipating the future as much as he was responding to the Holy Spirit deep within him. He was inviting God's power into the situation. Bill's "Hallelujah" was releasing God's Spirit to be at work, much in the same way that our prayers open the door and invite God to act.

This kind of shout comes from the Spirit at work within us. If encouraged to move in us, the Holy Spirit senses our moments of challenge and calls God's power into play. This only works if we are plugged into the source—and if we are willing to embrace the gift of strong emotion that God has given to us.

Of course, strong emotion can feel like a dangerous thing, especially when a long, difficult job search inspires difficult feelings of fear, anger, frustration, desperation, and despair. Squelching all emotion may seem easier than risking losing control of those negative feelings. But those deep emotions are part of how we were created. God fashioned us to experience the highs and lows of joy and grief, of love and loss, of laughter and tears. And if the Holy Spirit is here to inspire a shout of joy, the Spirit is also present to bring comfort and peace in times of anxiety.

Whatever emotion you may be feeling, let the Spirit marshal God's presence in your place of need. The Spirit prays better for you than you can for yourself; let our Advocate intercede on your behalf. And when you most need God's power, let out that "Hallelujah!" or shout "Amen!" with the Dominicans. Let that shout be a defiant proclamation of faith or a triumphant confirmation of victory. Through that burst of inexplicable joy, you are opening the path for God to enter and transform your situation. Amen!

One Small Step for Today

It is only logical that we will face some rejection before we find the right fit, but that logic is little comfort when rejection actually comes. The next time you get a discouraging letter or phone call, shout out a loud "Hallelujah," because you know that God is at work for his glory and your good. See if the Holy Spirit, who lives inside you, doesn't respond by refreshing you and rallying you against discouragement. Try it today!

What about Worry?

Do not be anxious about anything,
but in everything, by prayer and petition
with thanksgiving, present your requests
to God. And the peace of God which
transcends all understanding will guard
your hearts and minds in Christ Jesus.
—Philippians 4:6-7

This verse is the most difficult for me to put into practice and probably the most important in my everyday duties. I try to be responsible. I am on time. I keep my promises. I do my homework. In my work, I strive for the best, sacrificing for larger goals. Despite all this, I cannot control the outcome of every situation. No matter how many times I visualize a challenge to anticipate all possibilities, things happen that I do not expect.

I once saw a poster in a doctor's office that said, "You are not completely, irrevocably responsible for everything that happens. That is my job. —God." That is the issue for me. I have a problem remembering my place in the universe. This has caused me stress over the years and at times affected my health. That is why I need this verse. And I know I'm not alone!

God does not want us to worry. In the Sermon on the Mount, Jesus chides us for spending our energy worrying about the details of daily existence (Matthew 6). What has worry ever achieved for us other than stress, ulcers, wrinkles, and heart attacks? Besides, it is a terrible witness. In Matthew 6:32, Jesus points out that when we fret about the things of this world rather than trust God for them, we act as if we were unsaved ("for the pagans run after all these things"). Our trust in God's provision should reveal a marked difference between us and the rest of the world. When we worry, the message we send is that God cannot be trusted.

For those who, like me, struggle with an addiction to worry, let me suggest an exercise I call the "select and lift technique." It's a strategy to clamp down on worry. While it is not as good as dropping worry altogether, it can help wean you away from it. The first step is *select*: choose just one thing to worry about at a time instead of worrying about a million possibilities at once. Instead of visualizing the whole week ahead of you and worrying about all the things that could go wrong, focus on just one project or event—Tuesday's application deadline or Thursday's interview. Focus your energy on that and squeeze out all other nagging questions.

Step two is *lift*: lift the target worry to God in prayer. Do not try to deny your anxiety. Just confess, "Lord, I am worrying. I know I can't hold on to this worry and also be open to receive your joy in this situation, so help me to trade with you. You take the worry, and I'll take the joy." Try it. It's a good trade.

This two-step process may not totally cure your worrying—I'm still working on mine! If, however, you can recognize that worry is not what God wants for you, you can start exchanging your worries for the good stuff the Lord wants to give you instead.

One Small Step for Today

Practice the "select and lift" approach with your job search. Make a list of the things you are concerned about, such as perfecting your résumé, answering interview questions, paying your bills, acquiring key skills, and so on. Pick the most pressing one and focus on it, pushing all the rest of your concerns to another day. Consider the problem from several different angles, and then lift it to God. Admit your worry, and then open your hands and let go. Ask God to replace this worry with whatever you need for the next step of your search.

Faster Than a Speeding Bullet

*I have been very zealous for the LORD
God Almighty. . . . I am the only one left,
and now they are trying to kill me too.*
—1 Kings 19:10

In 1 Kings 19 we have a picture of the prophet Elijah at his worst. Just a chapter earlier, the Lord let Elijah save the day. Elijah said one prayer, and fire fell from heaven. The powerful fireworks display convinced the people of God's might, and Elijah destroyed his opposition. The prophet prayed again, and the long drought ended. Finally, Elijah, filled with the Spirit of God, did a "faster than a speeding bullet" routine and raced King Ahab's chariot to the city of Jezreel.

But even Superman has his weakness, and Elijah's kryptonite was the death threat that Jezebel sent him. Hadn't Elijah just achieved great victory in the Lord's name? Hadn't he proven that his God was more powerful than Jezebel's? But suddenly he was fleeing for his life. He wandered off into the desert, slouched under a tree, and turned on the drama. "I have had enough, LORD," he said. "Take my life; I am no better than my ancestors" (verse 4).

Like Elijah, we sometimes fall into despair. After a long struggle to serve God and provide for our families, the last straw comes in the form of what may otherwise seem to be a little rejection, a small disappointment, an easy-to-overcome obstacle. Maybe it is because we are trying to play Superman. We strive to guarantee ourselves success by doing everything right: polished résumé, impeccable interview suit, Web presence, LinkedIn profile, Facebook network. But deep down we all know that the Superman image is an illusion. We are not in control. The car breaks down on the way to an interview. We miss a call from a potential employer. We spill coffee on our new suit. Another candidate lands the dream job. Then we get asked a well-intended but spirit-sapping question: "No luck with the job hunt?"

Elijah's story illustrates how God works in our lives even in our darkest moments—even when we are inclined to wallow alone and in despair. Thank God for showing compassion and patience in those times! The Lord nourishes us, adjusts and restores our perspective, and finally gives us a task to get us moving forward again.

Playing Superman is fun, but when you eventually get knocked from the sky, the fall is shocking. Your loss of control may even make you question God's power and provision. It may cause you to forget the promises of Scripture and to neglect the lifeline of prayer. Thankfully, the Lord continues to send nourishment—whether through ravens (1 Kings 17:1-6), a poor widow (17:8-16), or the angels themselves (19:3-9). Keep welcoming this nourishment so that you will have strength to adjust when God shows up with a display of power and a new assignment.

When you catch yourself turning on the drama because of a small setback, rest up, eat well, and prepare for a fresh encounter with the Lord. It is God's way of reminding us that we don't need to be Superman; God is the one with the power and the resources to save the day.

One Small Step for Today

Your job search may be just the motivation you needed to get serious about daily Bible study. Just as the angel prepared food and water for Elijah before his journey up the mountain, God has given us Scripture to nourish our hearts. If you are going to be ready to hear what God has for you and follow the Spirit's guidance, you need to be well fed. Some of the Scriptures that have encouraged me are in the Psalms, the Gospel of John, and the epistles of Colossians and 1 Peter. God may lead you to others. Keep those verses close as you journey together with the Lord.

Out of Poverty

*Truly I tell you, this poor widow has put
more into the treasury than all the others.
They all gave out of their wealth; but she,
out of her poverty, put in everything—all
she had to live on.* —Mark 12:43-44

If you are applying for a first job or making a radical career switch,
you may feel like you don't have a lot to offer. You won't have a
wealth of experience or a portfolio of refined skills in the area you
are pursuing. Don't be discouraged! Remember, even the candidates with the best qualifications or the most experience are poor
in their own right; whether they admit it or not, they can only
offer employers what God has loaned them. It is our Creator God
who entrusts each of us with certain skills and allows us to enjoy
particular experiences.

That's the essence of Jesus' parable of the talents in Matthew
25. In first-century Judea, a talent was an amount of money—
roughly fifteen years' wages for a typical laborer. But today it
"translates" rather nicely that a talent is an innate gift or ability.
In the parable, a rich landowner goes on a journey and distributes
a share of his wealth to three servants, each with different lev-
els of ability. The most talented servant (we assume) receives the
largest share of the resources, with lesser shares being entrusted
to the other two.

The parable offers a multitude of lessons—about stewardship,
about fear, about trustworthiness, about rewards for good service—but the foundation of the story is that what we have comes
from God and we are responsible for managing our resources
wisely, with integrity, and with an awareness of the one to whom
those resources belong.

How does this relate to a sense of poverty in approaching the job search? Consider that if each of us comes to a prospective employer with nothing that God has not given to us, every one of us is poor in and of ourselves. And conversely, each one of us is also rich insofar as we possess the gifts that God has been generous to provide. Why should you feel more inadequate than anyone else when God is the one who equips us all?

Your responsibility is to manage wisely and give generously from whatever resources God first gave to you. The Lord has given you talents and dreams, so explore them. God has given you family and friends, so love and encourage them. God grants you energy and skills, so exercise them often and according to your own ability (see Matthew 25:15). Remember how pleased Jesus was with the widow's meager gift. And recall the master's words to his workers: "Well done, good and faithful servant! You have been faithful with a few things; I will put you in charge of many things. Come and share your master's happiness!" (Matthew 25:23).

Give your job search all that you have—however deep your well of resources may be. Reach for that position, even if you are not sure you are qualified. Perhaps God will give the employer eyes to perceive that you have given more than all the others—because you have given your all, even out of your relative poverty.

One Small Step for Today

Use a career development exercise called the STAR (or SAR) technique to identify the talents God has entrusted to you. Start by listing a situation (S) or task (T) in which you had to solve a problem. Then note the action (A) you took to resolve it, followed by the result (R). Use this formula in your résumé or interviews to demonstrate the practical, problem-solving application of specific skills you can offer. God has enriched you with more abilities than you may realize!

Roar

*Do not be overcome by evil, but overcome
evil with good.* —Romans 12:21

Our lives tend to be compartmentalized. We have work concerns,
which are separate from home concerns, which are separate from
church concerns. For each environment we have different sets of
unspoken rules. Somehow our brains cope better with a "divide
and conquer" strategy. But God does not belong in one of our
boxes; the Lord fills all of them. Your personal relationship with
God should permeate all parts of your life. God should go with
you into all settings, because you need the Lord in all settings.
Think of it this way: God is the source of perfection, and when
you invite the Lord into the midst of any endeavor, that task will
get a heavy push in the direction of goodness and excellence.

One of my favorite books is Bob Briner's *Roaring Lambs: A
Gentle Plan to Radically Change Your World*. Briner (1935–99)
was a television producer and sports manager with a huge impact on the profile of international sports, especially tennis and
basketball. However, Briner did not see his career as an end in
itself. As a Christian, Briner felt that he had a responsibility to
win a hearing for the Good News by demonstrating professional
excellence.

In *Roaring Lambs*, Briner encouraged all Christians, and especially those looking to enter the job market, to engage actively in
professions and activities that have maximum impact on culture.
He pointed to examples of people who have committed themselves to culture-shaping fields such as the media, politics, and the

arts, as well as individuals who are making a difference in their own communities. Briner also believed in encouraging young adults to enter these high-impact jobs rather than avoiding such fields because of their reputation for compromise.*

You don't have to work for a church or Christian organization to have a ministry or mission field. Not only are there many so-called secular fields that may encompass a call to ministry in the workplace—from social service careers and health-care professions to the education system and justice system. There are also organizations and entire professional fields that are desperate for the salt and light that just a few thoughtful Christians could bring. Often these are the very jobs we avoid.

If you have not yet found your true professional calling, pray about whether you may be gifted to work in a career that you would traditionally consider less than conducive to serving God. Ask the Lord to show you where you could have the biggest impact on our culture by bringing the Lord's goodness and excellence into that environment. In what positions could your skills make the most difference and would your "roar" be heard the most clearly?

One Small Step for Today

In his book *What Color Is Your Parachute?*, career guru Richard Bolles proposes that discovering your mission is about expressing love by bringing more truth, more beauty, or more perfection into the world. Bolles calls these three areas the Kingdom of the Mind, the Kingdom of the Heart, and the Kingdom of the Will.** Which of these three appeals most to you? Consider what culture-shaping fields would let you do this best.

---

*Bob Briner, *Roaring Lambs: A Gentle Plan to Radically Change Your World* (Grand Rapids: Zondervan, 1993).

**Richard Bolles, *What Color Is Your Parachute?* (Berkeley, Calif.: Ten Speed, 2005), 308.

The Greatness of Giving

Give, and it will be given to you. A good measure, pressed down, shaken together and running over, will be poured into your lap. For with the measure you use, it will be measured to you. —Luke 6:38

God does not intend for us to live under the constant pressure we often experience during a job search. This pressure is a product of the anxious human mind. Thankfully, God provides a way out of the unnecessary predicaments in which we place ourselves. One of the most effective remedies God offers is giving.

This cure was suggested to me by David, my closest friend through most of junior high and high school. During that time, David was not a believer. At times he was more of a skeptic, but God was working on his heart. After we graduated and went separate ways, David accepted Christ and gave himself to God with enthusiasm, eventually leaving with his family for missionary work in Siberia.

At a time when I was in the middle of a job search, David gave me a challenge. He suggested that when I felt overwhelmed, I should look for an opportunity to give to others exactly what I needed most myself. If my concern was money, I should give some away. If I was feeling rejected, I should look for someone I could affirm. If I felt isolated, I should reach out to someone lonely.

It made a strange kind of sense when I considered it. If I turn outward, I break my own concentration. It is like clapping your hands to startle someone who has been staring. Once we become conscious of the big picture, our problem is transformed from a looming giant into a squeaking mouse. The discipline has a spiritual dimension as well. By becoming channels through which God's love can flow to others, we also plug ourselves into God's order for the universe. The Lord's power courses through us again. Once we are reattached to our power source, God's power can work in the situation surrounding us.

I'm not suggesting that our service and generosity to others should have a self-serving agenda. We don't give to others just to get God to bless us. As we grow and mature in the Lord, we learn to give to others for the sake of doing what is good. Our giving becomes a way to restore God's desired order, and it is a sign that we have trusted God with our problems.

In his masterful work *Mere Christianity*, C. S. Lewis suggested that Christians are like actors donning a mask. Our mask is an imitation of Christ, and although we do not measure up to that image, if we wear the mask long enough, our faces may grow to fit its form.* Like an actor who always plays the same character, we also may come to internalize Christ's character and become like him. The right motivation for our performance may soon infuse us.

One Small Step for Today

Serving others at my own point of need has pulled me out of more than one funk in my job searches by reorienting my perspective toward giving rather than receiving. Try it! What is your most pressing concern—fear of failure, fear of rejection, or worry about providing for your family? How can you help someone else in the same area of need? Trust in Jesus' promise from Luke 6:38 and give knowing that God will take care of your needs.

*C. S. Lewis, *Mere Christianity* (1952; repr., New York: HarperCollins, 2001), 187.

Taking Your Medicine

Better is open rebuke than hidden love.
Wounds from a friend can be trusted,
but an enemy multiplies kisses.
—Proverbs 27:5-6

I had just finished my opening session with the search committee, and the committee chair was escorting me to the next round of my interview. As he led me down the hallway, he indicated the restrooms and suggested that this would be the right time for a stop. I agreed and headed for the door. My guide quietly added, "I think one of the tags is still on your suit."

I managed to say, "Oh, thanks." Inside the restroom, sure enough, I noticed a small, uncut cloth tag. I removed it carefully and went back out.

"Thanks again," I said.

"No problem. It's easy to miss those in a new suit. I thought you'd rather know."

You have probably had an experience like that, when you have been embarrassed when someone had to tell you that your pants were unzipped or you had food in your teeth. We may also receive painful feedback when it comes to talents and personal qualities. Sometimes we need someone to tell us that our people skills leave something to be desired, that we don't write as well as we think we do, or that we should invest in some breath mints. It can be tough to hear, but it would be worse if no one told us and we walked around like the kid with a "Kick me" sign on his back.

The job search is full of this kind of tough medicine. Maybe friends and relatives will pretend they don't see our weak spots, but employers will be looking for them. After a few résumés or interviews that fall flat, we may finally ask, "Do I need some improvement in this area?"

This is precisely when the Lord does the best work with us. When we start to realize that our own efforts and talents might not be enough, God knows we'll listen and be open to change. Sometimes God is the one to give us tough medicine, convicting us through Scripture or circumstance. At other times, God is the one to pick us up after we have been punched in the nose by some "constructive criticism." When we have just been crushed to learn that we don't really have the right stuff to fulfill our cherished dream, the Lord speaks to our hearts: "That's true, but it's okay. That's not why I love you. Besides, I have another plan for you, for my glory and your good."

While nobody likes taking such medicine, make the most of this unique time by being open to receiving what may help you. Maybe you'll get some honest advice that will spare you from pain later, or maybe God will dispel one dream only to give you a better one.

One Small Step for Today

My favorite exercise for assessing someone's strengths and weaknesses is called a 360-degree review. To get a robust view of how you are perceived and any blind spots you might not be aware of, identify people who can see you from different angles. Include someone who has supervised you, two or three colleagues or peers, and if possible, someone you have supervised or led in some way. Explain that you are conducting a strengths and weaknesses inventory and need their honest feedback. Ask each person a standard set of questions about what you do well and where you need work (see sample questions at www.aaronbasko.com). Compile their feedback. Typically you will discover one or more surprises you will want to know!

Stickers and Candy

> *Let the word of Christ dwell among you richly.* —Colossians 3:16

Did you attend Sunday school and memorize Bible verses for stickers and candy? Do you remember the verses now or just the candy? Or maybe what you remember most is not enjoying memorization.

In my class, we said a pledge to the Bible. The part that most stuck with me is "[I] will make it a lamp unto my feet and a light unto my path. And I will hide its words in my heart that I might not sin against God." It has taken me years to understand and appreciate what "hide . . . in my heart" meant. Well, basically it took me until my first big job search.

The verse I stumbled on during that season of my life was James 1:12, which declares, "Blessed is the one who perseveres under trial because, having stood the test, that person will receive the crown of life that the Lord has promised to those who love him." The verse resonated strongly with me because that first job hunt was a long and frustrating one. I needed to cling to the promise in these words—and that meant keeping them always in mind and close to heart.

Now I know that this verse was written in the context of great persecution. The first-century church had been scattered across the Roman Empire, opposed both by the Jews and the Romans. People who were discovered to be followers of Christ were subject to beatings, imprisonment, confiscation of lands, and even execution. Most of us won't ever see that kind of persecution for our faith.

Still, reading that verse reminded me of God's sovereignty and encouraged me that whatever the level of challenge, God promises to bring good out of it. During my job search, I read it, reread it, and read it again. I could recite it without hesitation—and did so often. I didn't receive any gold stars or candy for memorizing it; I was just glad to know where to find its assurance when I needed it!

Over the years, I have identified several favorite verses, including Galatians 5:1; 1 Peter 1:13; and 1 John 5:12. As each new major challenge presents itself, the Holy Spirit seems to bring a new Scripture that becomes a part of me. Now I seek them out as if finding a walking stick for the trail or a flashlight on a dark night. Having the right reminders of God's promises and power can make all the difference on those darkest days. Those memory verses become candy for your soul.

One Small Step for Today

Do you have a favorite Scripture verse? If you have never asked God for one, ask and keep your eyes open as you read your Bible. Perhaps there is some passage that calls to your heart every time you read it, like a promise that God has spoken to you. Keep such a verse close to your heart. Place it on a card inside your interview folder or on the dashboard of your car. Pray it back to the Lord when you need special encouragement. Whether you find a favorite for life or just a new verse for this season, hide it in your heart and delight in it often.

Plan for Praise

I will give thanks to you, LORD, *with all
my heart; I will tell of all your wonderful
deeds. I will be glad and rejoice in you;
I will sing the praises of your name, O
Most High.* —Psalm 9:1-2

Are you praising God during this challenging job search time?
Humankind was created to give God glory. If we do not praise
our Creator, we rob ourselves of a tremendous power supply.
Consider that praise is to our spiritual health what laughter is to
physical health. Both have amazing restorative and healing benefits—laughter for the body, praise for the soul.

I don't always feel like laughing. But isn't that often the time
when I most need to laugh? So what do I do? I give it a little help.
For me, enticing laughter means spending time with my kids—
wrestling, playing hide-and-seek, or watching a funny movie. I
find something in our play to spark that laughter. I also try to
spend time around other people who love to laugh, because I
know laughter is contagious.

It is the same with praise. When I do not feel like praising but
I know that I need it, I make a plan to get to a place where I can
praise. That place may or may not include church on Sunday
morning. When I really want to connect with God, I often have
to go intentionally beyond my normal setting. Sometimes that
means withdrawing to a place of special beauty, going for a solitary run, or taking a long drive accompanied by God and some
great music. Wherever I go to find that place of praise, my inten-
tion is to discover myself in God's presence.

The Lord has been very gracious to me. I remember that during the toughest days of my first job search, I attended a men's

conference with my dad and two other guys. The conference was huge, and at one point I found myself surrounded by thousands of men singing (bellowing is a better description) and rejoicing in a way I had never experienced. That event helped restore the proper perspective to my life. I could see that God's purpose for me was much bigger than my job search and that God was infinitely greater that my situation.

The Lord has arranged that kind of experience for me several times when I really needed it. God and I have met on the shore of a loch in Scotland, at a concert at Red Rocks in Colorado, and on a camping trip with my sons and a small group of guys. Each time the experience was in response to an invitation. In each case, I had the opportunity to say no. By God's grace, however, I accepted each invitation as it came. And each time, despite the challenges that plagued me, the Lord gave me an amazing reason to praise.

When we praise, we purposefully acknowledge the perfect order of God's universe. We are plugged into a worldview that includes multitudes of God's children, the hosts of heaven, and the God who is the definition of the word *power*. When we praise, the electricity of God's creation courses through us. Plan for times of praise. They will elevate your view and remind you that God is very much in control.

One Small Step for Today

God will surprise you by arranging spontaneous times for you to connect with the Holy Spirit in praise, but you also need to plan for such times. Praising God and restoring proper order to your universe is vital. Include it in your job search by penciling some time into your planning calendar, at least once every other week. This is time specifically for praise, not petition. Set aside an hour (or more) without distractions and plug back into your divine power supply.

"Don't Think, Wally!"

> *Finally brothers and sisters, whatever is*
> *true, whatever is noble, whatever is right,*
> *whatever is pure, whatever is lovely, what-*
> *ever is admirable—if anything is excellent*
> *or praiseworthy, think about such things.*
> —Philippians 4:8

All of our extended family lived far away as I was growing up, so my parents formed an "adopted" family from friends in our church and neighborhood. One of the most important adopted family members in my life was a longtime neighbor named Josephine, whom I called "Grammy Jo." Grammy Jo was the neighborhood mother. She kept an eye on everyone on our street, and if someone's party got too loud or she saw drag racers on our otherwise quiet road, she would bake the offender a chocolate cake to let that person know she knew.

Grammy Jo was fiercely proud of being Irish, and her love of fun and mischief always made us wonder if she was part leprechaun. Not only did she throw the best St. Patrick's Day parties north of Boston, but her great sense of humor kept everyone around her off guard. Even in her eighties, she was an incurable flirt, an ace at cards, and a great dancer.

Grammy Jo never seemed to let things get her down for very long—especially something she deemed to be as useless as worry. While her husband was alive, the two of them teased each other constantly. I remember how she would get a plan set in her mind, and he would start to bring up possible problems. He would play devil's advocate just to get her worked up, smiling the whole time. Finally, she would get exasperated and say, "Don't talk, Wally!

Don't think." It was her way of tuning out the doubt and refusing to let him frustrate her. She would just focus on what she needed to do to bring her latest impossible plan to inevitable fruition.

As a child, I was awed by Grammy Jo, but as an adult, I have a tendency to function more like her beloved husband. Even when the idea is my own, my mind is prone to wander, and I have a knack for second-guessing myself. I amaze myself with the time and creativity I can invest in playing out possible scenarios in my head. *What if this happens? What if that doesn't come through? How can I be prepared for every possibility?*

Why is it so difficult to think on the true, the noble, and the pure? I have to remind myself to tune out the voices of skepticism, doubt, and fear, but it isn't easy. I have to imitate Grammy Jo and say to those questions, "Don't talk!" and say to myself, "Don't think!"

At one point in a job search, I told a friend that I had been spending a lot of time thinking about what God wanted me to do. "Why have you wasted all that time?" he replied. "You could be following God's will today instead." Rather than wasting time thinking about things that may or may not ever happen, we should focus on what God gives us to do each day.

"Don't think, Wally!"

One Small Step for Today

Make a list of all the aspects of your job search over which you have little control. Pretty big list, right? So why are you spending time trying to control those things? If you have some kind of in-box or file where you keep your new job search–related information, make a second one and label it for God. Then take the list of things you can't control and put it in God's box. Now list those things you can control, and start working on those.

This Might Get Bumpy

Who knows but that you have come
to your royal position for such a time
as this? —Esther 4:14

As I speak with other Christians about their career experiences, I'm awed by how frequently they recount situations that would be unexplainable without God. I have come to think of those kinds of experiences as roller-coaster turns. Here you are moving along the track of your career and life when suddenly God takes the car around a sharp curve or down a steep drop. The Lord knows that the car is on the track, but the g-force is making your stomach do flip-flops. For a moment, you are sure you are about to go careening off the track.

On a ride it is fun to feel a little out of control, but the roller-coaster turns we experience in life are not quite as enjoyable. To us they feel like unexpected jolts and unwelcome shocks. The abrupt turns seem accidental, but God is not surprised.

Think of Queen Esther. The Sunday school version goes like this: orphan girl lives with her uncle, enters the royal beauty pageant, wins the crown, and bravely approaches the king to expose the villain and save her people. The real biblical story reads more like a life-or-death version of the reality show *The Bachelor*. Required to leave her home, Esther is confined in luxury for a year for a one-shot date with the king, a man whose advances she can't refuse. Even if she doesn't wow the king, she can't go home; she'll be relegated to the harem. She has no freedom in this high-stakes game.

When chosen as queen, Esther should be able to live happily ever after. Instead, she is soon embroiled in a dangerous court intrigue. An anonymous Jew in the Persian court, Esther finds herself flung around a hairpin turn when a royal adviser convinces the king to commit genocide against the Jews. Does she dare expose herself and risk the king's wrath by protesting the holocaust, or should she keep silent and watch her people be destroyed? From her uncle's viewpoint, Esther is in exactly the right position for God's glory to shine through her.

As I wrote this entry, I was coaching a recent graduate searching for a first job. Starting out in a slow job market, especially without any real experience, was tough for this student. On top of that, she had realized her degree was in a field she didn't really like. A little like Esther, trying to transition from trophy wife to Jewish ambassador, the student was facing the need to forge a path in a different direction and to convince employers that she had the transferable skills to make a contribution.

I encouraged her then as I encourage you now: God is opening and closing unseen doors for you. That is hard to accept when all you feel is the g-force of that roller-coaster turn. Esther felt it too, but with a little help she realized that God had been preparing her for "such a time as this." Trust that God knows the curves in the track and is preparing you to face them.

One Small Step for Today

Esther "won the favor" of the king and of "everyone who saw her" (Esther 2:15). She understood the importance of treating everyone with respect. This principle has direct applications to the job search. Treat every person you meet in the process with courtesy, from the secretary to the CEO. Do not underestimate proper protocol, from sending thank-you notes to addressing people by (the correct and correctly spelled) name. Buy some quality note cards and work out a system for accurately capturing the names of the people you meet in your search process. Win some favor!

Sweet Dreams

For the Spirit God gave us does not make us timid, but gives us power, love and self-discipline. —2 Timothy 1:7

Hershey, Pennsylvania, is one of my family's favorite places on earth. My wife introduced me to Hershey's Chocolate World when we were dating, and since then we have made many pilgrimages to the town with streetlights shaped like Hershey Kisses and the smell of warm chocolate in the air. We have tried out the Kissing Tower, attended concerts, and visited the botanical gardens and the zoo, and we have pictures of our kids with every Hershey's candy character. In fact, we rode the Chocolate World factory ride the day before my daughter was due to be born. We had fun imagining my wife going into labor on the ride and being rewarded with a lifetime supply of chocolate! There is just something magical about Hershey.

This amazing place, which has sweetened the lives of people around the world, exists because of one man who was not afraid to fail. Milton Hershey was acquainted with business failures. His father, Henry Hershey, was a poor entrepreneur whose constant pursuit of his next business scheme caused the family to move frequently. Milton himself started two candy-making businesses, one in Philadelphia and one in New York City, both of which failed, leaving him penniless. He started a third candy business, and after some initial difficulties, began to make a profit. Eventually Hershey became wealthy from his Lancaster Caramel Company, but in 1900 he sold it to pursue a new dream of creating a milk chocolate factory that would become the largest in the world.*

Milton Hershey did not let the fear of failure prevent him from achieving greatness. We all have had bad past experiences. It is tempting to let these events rule us and warp how we approach major life decisions like the job search. After being burned, we think, "I'm never letting that happen again!" We let our world get smaller because we are determined never to get hurt. Like an athlete whose injury develops into a scar that prevents the full range of motion, we fear repeating our mistakes and seeing ourselves as failures.

I have my own set of scars, and I have to be vigilant lest they inhibit my decision making. When I find myself thinking fearfully about the past, I have to stop and invite God into the situation. The question to answer before going any further is, "What is my definition of success and failure?" Only you, with God and a few select, wise counselors, get to decide what events qualify as successes or failures. That unexpected bump in your past is only a failure if you define it as one—and get stuck there. Let it become a teaching tool in the hands of your God.

So if you find yourself battling worries about failure, think about Milton Hershey's journey. Remember that you may be only one bad experience away from sweet success.

One Small Step for Today

A friend of mine who speaks to college and high school groups likes to ask, "What would you do if it were impossible to fail?" Playing it safe in a job search is easy, but this may be a time to be bold. Embrace the risk and let it fuel your creativity. What is it that God has written on your heart to do? What would the work look like? Could you get paid to do something like this—maybe not tomorrow, but in time? What steps could you take in a next job to get you closer?

*Millie Landis Coyle, "Milton Snavely Hershey," Hershey-Derry Township Historical Society, www.hersheyhistory.org/library-archives/hershey/54-milton-snavely-hershey (accessed May 14, 2012).

Getting (More Than)
What We Deserve

You can make many plans, but the LORD'S purpose will prevail. —Proverbs 19:21, NLT

We live in a culture of entitlement. We have more money and freedom than most of the world can imagine, and we grow up feeling entitled to most of it. Parents want their children to have the best life has to offer, and they use money, connections, and influence to help them attain those goals. After having food, clothing, shelter, entertainment, transportation, education, and more provided from birth, many of us experience a rude awakening upon entering the workaday world. Facing that first job search may be the first time some people realize they really aren't as entitled as they have always assumed. A feeling of entitlement is just that: a feeling, not a reality.

Working in higher education, I see entitlement in action often. I try not to judge because I have been there myself. Parents feel they are entitled to have the government or the college pay their costs. Students feel entitled to a guarantee of a good job when they graduate. Such a sense of entitlement only makes life more stressful after graduation. Despite all the messages we may hear from grade school through college commencement, having the right education, the right awards, the right family or community connections, or the right power suit for the first interview—none of it is a guarantee of the perfect job or even a living wage.

"But I've earned it. I deserve it. I worked hard to get here. Where are my just deserts?" These are the cries of entitlement. Their voices are familiar, but they are illusory. In the job search, it is crucial not to buy into the message of entitlement that surrounds us. If we do, we are either feeding our pride or simply lying to ourselves. Better to prepare ourselves with the challenging recognition that no one owes us anything—not God and certainly not the stranger sitting across the interview table. Everything we have, including the favor we find with prospective employers, comes from God.

Friends will attempt to encourage you by saying, "With that background, you'll find a job with no problem." Don't fall for the well-intentioned hype. Don't allow yourself to trust in a feeling of entitlement. Trust instead that you have been created for a purpose by God and that God alone has guaranteed your eternal inheritance. Know that God's plan and purpose for you are unfolding at this very moment. And if your trust is in the Lord, you may be confident that the Holy Spirit is even now working out a plan for you and that it is much, much bigger than today's job search. (To know just how big, read Ephesians 1:4-14 again and again.)

One Small Step for Today

God has put people in your life who know both you and the field you want to enter. They can give you a realistic, rather than entitled, view of your skills. These are the people you want as your references. They will be excellent advocates and sounding boards for you, so keep them informed of your process. Tell them when you are interviewing, if they are likely to be contacted, and how you are approaching the position. Create a professional-looking reference list that includes complete contact information, and bring hard copies to any interview.

Mystery Machine

Can you fathom the mysteries of God?
Can you probe the limits of the Almighty?
—Job 11:7

My wife does not like surprises. It took me ten years of marriage to realize that the smartest thing for me to do is to buy her exactly what she has on her list. God has a sense of humor, because I'm a spontaneous and romantic guy, and for years I tried to outdo myself by surprising her with the right gift. Finally, she clued me in. Now I just ask her for the specifics.

I, on the other hand, love surprises. I am better off if I don't make a Christmas list. Without one, I can just enjoy the surprise. If my kids and I are sharing candies or popsicles or some other treat, they'll ask which kind I want, and I'll typically say, "Surprise me!" I like the adventure of not knowing every detail—at least when I know the surprise is a good one.

When it comes to something more serious, however, such as job change, I have always seen the element of surprise differently. Somehow my concern for control kicks in, and what once seemed adventurous now looks a little scary. And yet when I read in the Bible about people like Daniel or Rebekah or Paul, I see that one of the most exciting things about walking with God is the constant sense of mystery as the Holy Spirit reveals God's plan in my life.

Have you ever seen the animated television show, *Scooby Doo?* Scooby Doo is a cartoon Great Dane who sort of talks. He and his human buddy, Shaggy, travel around with a band of misfit friends in an outlandishly painted van that they call the "Mystery Machine," solving crimes and unraveling mysteries. Invariably, their mysteries involve some kind of spooky monster or ghost that terrifies Scooby and Shaggy but is ultimately unmasked as a flesh-and-blood human being in disguise.

Following God's plan is a lot like riding around in the Mystery Machine. We never know quite what adventure will befall us. We run into unexpected monsters that loom over us, but because we are traveling in good company, the monsters are eventually unmasked and lose their power. By the end, the fear turns back into adventure.

I want to walk in the mystery of God. I read Paul's words in Ephesians 1:9, "He made known to us the mystery of his will according to his good pleasure, which he purposed in Christ," and I see that the mysteriousness of God has great purpose. God is a mystery to my limited brain, but the longer I walk with the Lord, the clearer it becomes that God's mystery is for my good. God's Spirit is someone real with whom I can walk, anticipate, and delight in. Each time I face a new chapter of my future, I want to step into the Mystery Machine to see what adventure God has planned for the two of us together.

One Small Step for Today

A good mystery empowers us to figure out a puzzle. Approach your job search as a mystery. When you have identified the particular organizations you want to target, become a "mystery shopper" to learn as much as you can about them. Buy their products and interact with their personnel. Ask other "shoppers" about their experience with the organization. Your "mystery shopper" activity will make you aware of the needs of the organization and suggest how to present yourself as a solution to those needs.

Do-Gooders

Let us not become weary in doing good, for at the proper time we will reap a harvest if we do not give up. Therefore, as we have the opportunity, let us do good to all people, especially to those who belong to the family of believers. —Galatians 6:9-10

In my various positions, I have a lot of requests from young professionals who want to talk with me about getting started in my field. I always try to honor these requests. I enjoy helping others with professional development, and it is a way to pass on the help that I received in my job search. At first such encounters might feel awkward. Two people agree to a meeting, or one offers to take the other out for lunch. The initial interaction is sometimes tense; the young person is nervous, and the "expert" may be wary and watchful of time. In the best-case scenario, however, both people are willing to be there and interested in making the most of the encounter.

Of course, not all networking overtures are well received. Not all requests for expert information are granted graciously. Have you ever had a potential contact slam the door in your face, or have you been rushed off the phone by someone who was clearly not paying much attention to your questions anyway? It happens to all of us at some point. The question is, how will you let it affect you?

Feeling defensive is normal when you are not on sure footing in life, and it is human nature to want to strike back when you feel frustrated. In the Sermon on the Mount, however, Jesus counsels us not to repay evil with evil, but with good. It isn't an easy teaching, but it does make sense from God's perspective. When someone wrongs me and I strike back, either at that person or someone else, what happens? I have doubled the amount of evil that came into the world from that wrong. The evil was passed to me like an infectious disease, and I helped it multiply.

Contrast this with what happens if I repay evil with good. First I stop the evil from spreading. Not only do I keep myself from getting infected, but I might start the offender on the road to health. By God's grace, the germ finds nothing to feed on. Instead, I give it a dose of astringent goodness.

When given the choice between doing evil and doing good, be a do-gooder. Do not let the disappointments of your search make you bitter toward others. Give graciously of yourself during this time, and the joy you find will buoy your confidence and your sense of purpose. Consider how your responses could trigger a chain reaction of positive interactions that could come full circle to you when you need its benefits most. Allow God to use you to bring more goodness into the world.

One Small Step for Today

Informational interviewing is a powerful tool in the job search process. Find someone who works in a field that interests you, and ask for a meeting. You are not asking for a job or for any awkward favors. Ask questions about the field and about what you can do to be a compelling candidate. Ask the individual to take a look at your résumé and help you think like an insider in the field. If the person is a Christian, solicit prayers for your success. You will learn a remarkable amount, and in most cases the other person will be happy to become your ally.

On Mission

So we fix our eyes not on what is seen,
but on what is unseen, since what is seen
is temporary, but what is unseen is eternal.
—2 Corinthians 4:18

Taking a line from the film *Mission Impossible*, "Your mission, should you choose to accept it" is to live in two worlds in your career. One world is the concrete, visible world around you. It includes paychecks and taxes, emails and phone calls, tools and vehicles. This is the world in which your goal is to complete tasks and measure results in order to earn a living and strengthen a company or organization.

The other world you live in is largely intangible and relational. It includes the people around you and your role in advancing the reign of God on earth. In this second world, your goal is to use your influence to make your corner of the world resemble what God intends for it, primarily through sharing the love of God with others in word and deed.

Make no mistake: the second world is the most important. Within a year, everyone at your job may forget that amazing event you coordinated or those sales goals you met, but if you influence the people you work with for Christ, then you change history forever. Your double life in the unseen world is also more dangerous. You'll face the constant temptation to forget who you are. Just as the apostle Paul spent time "undercover" as a tent maker, your temporary assignment may be as a janitor, an accountant, a chef, or an insurance adjuster, but your true identity is that of a child of God.

As a job hunter, think of yourself as being in the preparation stages of your next mission. What special training will God give you during this time? What equipment will you need? Now is the time to practice thinking in your dual identity and to pray about how you can honor God in your mission field, wherever it may be.

It is easy to get distracted by the worries and cares that a job brings, but you must never forget the mission. Others will be watching you, especially if they get the sense that something is different about you. You are God's (not-so) secret agent—the Lord's way of penetrating the most unlikely places with the love of Jesus. Be ready to point to God as the difference-maker in your life, and be very careful not to elevate what is temporary (your everyday work) over what is eternal (the people God puts in your path).

Just as in *Mission Impossible*, the Lord has been carefully preparing your assignment ahead of time and has selected you as the right person for the job. God is using this time to help you understand the big mission for your life, even as you discover the smaller day-to-day mission that will be your next assignment. You will have to unravel many mysteries, but God believes you are the right agent for this impossible mission—if you choose to accept it.

One Small Step for Today

In almost every interview process, you will have an opportunity to highlight who you are and what value you believe you will bring to the organization. That may be a chance to share your "mission possible." Knowing what you want to convey will help you be ready when the moment comes. Sometimes the employer will ask you a question that allows you to answer with your mission answer. At other times you will sense a moment of quiet expectation, often near the end of the interview process. Be ready for it.

How to Outwrestle Samson

Do not let loyalty and faithfulness
forsake you; bind them around your
neck, write them on the tablet of your
heart. So you will find favor and good
repute in the sight of God and of people.
—Proverbs 3:3-4, NRSV

When I was young, one of my favorite heroes of the Bible was Samson. I marveled at his strength and great exploits, but as I grew older, I began to see how flawed Samson's character was. He had been given so much. He could have been one of Israel's most effective leaders, freeing them from all Philistine threats.

But Samson never sought his purpose. He never seemed concerned about the greater good of the nation or God's plan. Instead, he struck back when he was angry and chased after whatever woman caught his eye. God did use Samson, with all his flaws, to create havoc for Israel's enemies, but consider how much more Samson could have accomplished if he had pursued God's work or been passionate for God's people. Because of his supernatural strength and easy success, Samson never had to develop good character. He made his first small step toward character growth only right before he died, when all his strength was gone.

With a little help from the Holy Spirit, your character could wrestle Samson's to the ground any day. That should be an encouragement as you search for the right position. It will be tempting at times to focus on short-term victory or pleasures, but do not lose sight of those qualities that show that you are part of God's family. As Proverbs 3 reminds us, the traits of love and faithfulness must be part of who we are, not domestic habits that we drop as soon as we enter the "world of work."

Character is formed by consistent behavior, by writing love and faithfulness "on the tablet of your heart" and carrying them with you. As you apply for positions and seek interviews, you will naturally want to seem like the perfect candidate. You are trying to show the employer only your best face (or a better mask!)—while that employer is trying to detect any inconsistencies behind that interview façade. Unfortunately, this dynamic is one reason that many people end up in the wrong position and why so many employers and employees continue to consider each other adversaries from the employee's first day on the job.

Don't bother with the pretense. Employers are looking for consistency; show them that love and faithfulness (as well as hard work) follow you wherever you go. Let those with whom you network, and even those who seem to have nothing to do with your job search, see the character God is building in you. Rather than a desperate job seeker, people will see consistency and integrity, and "you will gain favor and good repute in the sight of God and of people."

One Small Step for Today

Prepare for a successful interview by identifying a list of common interview questions (easy to find online) and writing out your answers in advance. Then, when asked these common questions, you can focus on connecting with your audience instead of fumbling your way through the answer. As you prepare your answers, consider what they say about your character. Are you saying what you think your audience wants to hear, or are you projecting your best, but honest, self? Go for honesty.

Scheduled Maintenance

Wait for the LORD; *be strong and*
take heart and wait for the LORD.
—Psalm 27:14

I'm a pretty impatient person. (If you have much work experience, you know the type. I sent you an email to check on a project, but I'm outside your door asking you about it before the email gets to you.) When I'm working in my own strength, I'm a get-it-done person. I move through projects quickly. I like my inbox clean and my to-do list done. That kind of focus serves me well at the early stages of a job search, as I research like a maniac, build my network, and fine-tune my résumé. As the search drags on, however, I am tempted to act rashly.

The biblical stories of such rashness are not pretty. Consider the example in the book of 1 Samuel, where King Saul faces a critical moment in his young reign. The Philistine armies are arrayed against him, and the Israelite men are hiding in caves, quaking in fear. The standoff lasts seven days, at which point the prophet Samuel has promised to come to make the usual sacrifices before the army goes into battle. But Samuel is late, and the men are starting to desert. So Saul rashly makes the sacrifices himself—too impatient to wait for his mentor, who arrives while the altar fires are still smoking.

Samuel is not happy—and he makes it clear that neither is God. "You have done a foolish thing. You have not kept the command the LORD your God gave you; if you had, he would have established your kingdom over Israel for all time. But now your kingdom will not endure" (1 Samuel 13:13-14). Saul's impatience was the first nail in the coffin of his reign.

In such times of waiting, it is as if the Lord is taking us offline for scheduled maintenance. We need these times when we are forced to wait because our own efforts make little difference. God is actually doing some important work during these interludes, building our dependence and trust and arranging vital details around us. But instead of appreciating the Lord's efforts on our behalf, we are like little kids who fuss about going to bed because we think our bodies will be bored when we are asleep.

Each time that I have waited for God to provide the opportunity, I found a good job on the other side. The only job that I did not like was my first, which I accepted because I felt as if I had no options. While God was gracious enough to use that rash error in judgment, I can't help but wonder what might have happened if I had waited a little longer and trusted a bit more.

Instead of viewing this job search as wasted time, learn to wait actively. Seek to engage with what God is doing in your life. Pray for a clearer view of what lessons the Lord is teaching you and for the wisdom to be a quick and thorough learner. Get better at being still and listening for the guidance of the Holy Spirit. Wait eagerly and with assurance that after the scheduled maintenance, God's program will be seen more clearly than ever.

One Small Step for Today

Impatience is often self-centered, the result of assuming our time and our agenda are more important than those of others. Pop culture may encourage us to see other people as means to our own ends, but that is not God's perspective. While you are actively waiting for the Lord, practice being present to the people around you. Partner with God in the waiting process by practicing empathy over efficiency and engaging conversation over conflict. Stop rushing and start really living in the moments you have.

Tighten Your Grip

> *Now choose life, so that you and your*
> *children may live, and that you may love*
> *the LORD your God, listen to his voice,*
> *and hold fast to him. For the LORD is*
> *your life.* —Deuteronomy 30:19-20

So what happens when your tough job search pays off and you receive an offer that is a fit? As you look back, you can see how the Lord walked with you through every step of the process. God has taught you some things about yourself as you have been tested by the waiting, searching, and stretching. The Holy Spirit has probably taught you more about God as well. Hopefully during this time you have come to better understand the heart of the Lord for you.

But what now? As you proceed into the next phase of your professional life, will you look back at your job search as a "camp experience," which makes you feel good when you think of it but doesn't permanently change the way you live? Or will this time of walking with the Lord be the big leap forward in your life that leads to a new way of seeing your work and living it out for God? Did this journey provide the help you wanted merely for the job search, or has it offered the help you will draw upon throughout the months and years to come? Now is the moment to tighten your grip on the lessons you have learned. Follow Jacob's lead, and don't let go until you have received the full blessing for the wrestling you have done.

One of my job changes required my family to relocate about three hours away. My employer wanted me to start right away, but we had a house to sell and kids in school. For about six weeks, I spent the workweek in the new town, staying in temporary housing, and traveled back and forth on the weekends. To get a strong jump start on my work in the new position, for the first few weeks I worked thirteen-hour days plus making a forty-five-minute commute each way. The days were long, and I missed my family, but I kept my grip on the Lord.

I was sure that God had led me to this new post, and I wanted the Lord to be a part of everything I did in this new adventure. I soon realized that, although it was difficult in many ways, this time was another huge blessing for me, as it allowed me to focus on just two things: my new work and the Lord's voice. My weekday and weekend commutes gave me time to pray and prepare at the start and end of my day. My solitary weeknights gave me just enough time to eat while I read my Bible. I learned to relish what God was teaching me there.

Don't relax your dependency on the Lord when a job opportunity arrives. Hold on tighter! Maintain that spiritual sensitivity that you developed during your search. As you begin a new position, pray that God will grant you wisdom to see where you fit in the organization. Ask the Lord to continue to be your compass and your shield as you continue down this new road. Remember the promise in Jeremiah 29:11 about God's good plan for you, and take heart from 1 Thessalonians 5:24 that "the one who called you is faithful, and he will do it."

One Small Step for Today

As you move forward, continue to practice the good habits you established in your job search—both spiritual and professional. For instance, especially in the first few weeks, take the same good notes you took during informational interviews, highlighting names and procedures you learn. Be faithful in your patterns of prayer and Bible reading. Regularly update your portfolio of accomplishments with your new work. Above all else, keep believing that your experiences are for God's glory and your good.

Afterword

If you have just finished reading the meditations in this book, know that I have been praying for you and your job search. Beginning this book was one of God's many demonstrations of grace to me in my own job hunt. Ever since, I have prayed that God's grace will also reach out to others who want help in their job search. Before you even opened this volume, I prayed for victory in your search and that your relationship with God will be deepened by this challenging time.

If you have found a position where God wants you right now, I hope this book was a blessing along the way. Now share it with someone else. Remember the trust you have been building with the Lord. It will serve you well in your new position. Don't let it get away!

If you are still in the search process, be encouraged. If you are faithfully seeking wisdom and God's will, you can be confident that God is preparing the perfect spot for you. Your joy will be doubly rich because of the meticulous care God is taking to prepare you and those with whom you will work. Remember, your heavenly Headhunter always works for your best interest. Reread the parts of this book that were most meaningful to you. Then do what I did when my search began to grow long: ask God to bring something wonderful out of your challenge—even if it is just a small step for today.

My prayers are with you as you make your big leap. And I trust that this thin volume provided some of the help you wanted along the way.